IT Architecture
Toolkit

ENTERPRISE COMPUTING SERIES

IT Architecture Toolkit

Jane A. Carbone

 Prentice Hall PTR, Upper Saddle River, NJ 07458
http://www.phptr.com

Library of Congress Cataloging-in-Publication Data

Editorial/Production Supervision: *Mary Sudul*
Acquisitions Editor: *Gregory G. Doench*
Editorial Assistant: *Raquel Kaplan*
Marketing Manager: *Debby vanDijk*
Manufacturing Manager: *Alexis R. Heydt-Long*
Cover Design Direction: *Jerry Votta*
Cover Design: *Talar Boorujy*
Series Design: *Gail Cocker-Bogusz*

© 2004 Prentice Hall PTR
Prentice-Hall, Inc.
A Simon & Schuster Company
Upper Saddle River, NJ 07458

Prentice Hall books are widely used by corporations and government agencies for training, marketing, and resale.

The publisher offers discounts on this book when ordered in bulk quantities.
For more information, contact Corporate Sales Department, Phone: 800-382-3419; fax: 201-236-7114; email: corpsales@prenhall.com or write Corporate Sales Department, Prentice Hall PTR, One Lake Street, Upper Saddle River, NJ 07458.

Printed in the United States of America

6th Printing

ISBN 0-13-147379-4

Pearson Education LTD.
Pearson Education Australia PTY, Limited
Pearson Education Singapore, Pte. Ltd
Pearson Education North Asia Ltd
Pearson Education Canada, Ltd.
Pearson Educación de Mexico, S.A. de C.V.
Pearson Education — Japan
Pearson Education Malaysia, Pte. Ltd
Pearson Education, Upper Saddle River, New Jersey
Editora Prentice-Hall do Brasil, Ltda., *Rio de Janeiro*

Table of Contents

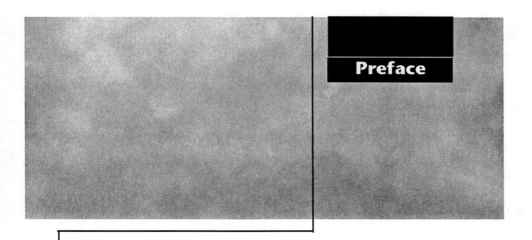

There were two factors that motivated me to write this book. One was that, while those of us who were *data geeks* were always passionate about business information, our opinions were not always popular. Today, meaningful, accurate information is the lifeblood of most organizations. In fact, in many cases, information is not just critical to the business—it *is* the business. Therefore, the need to plan how data is collected, flows through the organization, and is transformed into information the business can access, is vital. That need is increasingly recognized, not only by CIOs, but also by CEOs and even by the non-IT world at large. I was pleasantly surprised to read the following in an unlikely source:

> Halfway through the last century, information became a thing. It became a commodity, a force—a quantity to be measured and analyzed. It's what our world runs on. Information is the gold and the fuel.
> (James Glieck, "Bit Player," *The New York Times Magazine*, December 30, 2001)

The second factor that motivated me to write this book was that, just as a converted smoker becomes overly eager about the smoking habits of those around him, I have had my own *religious experience*. Having been honed (some would say charred) on the altar of architecture, I am eager to share both my suffering and my successes. Having learned many lessons the hard way, I am anxious to help you benefit from those lessons.

This book, therefore, is a very practical guide to enterprise architecture. Many fine minds have addressed architecture theory from the podium and the bookshelf. The purpose of this book is to help architects, IT planners, and analysts find ways to implement those theories, and to spare you as much pain as possible in the process.

Frequently Asked Questions

1. Q. Is this just more theory?

    A. No. The Toolkit is very practical—it is based on our learnings as chief architects and consultants (and in both cases, compensation was determined by success).

2. Q. How can you ensure that business needs are addressed in the architecture?

    A. Having wrestled with this problem, we developed a business framework and methods for translating business needs to architecture outputs. The Toolkit also addresses financial considerations and measurement development to tightly link architecture with the business.

3. Q. How does this approach relate to the Zachman Framework for Enterprise Architecture?

    A. The Toolkit architecture framework produced by our company, infomajic, is consistent with, but simpler than, the Zachman Framework. It focuses on the upper left-hand rows and provides methods for filling in the cells. It also addresses strategies for implementing target architecture. The Toolkit is very practical—it's based on experience. We'll do a more complete comparison with the Zachman Framework a little later.

4. Q. How do you create architecture outputs?

    A. We discuss what the critical outputs are—principles, models, inventory, and standards—and include specific methods for developing them. Examples and exercises allow you to practice using them.

5. Q. Does the Toolkit address "soft" issues, like getting business buy-in for architecture?

    A. Yes. The Toolkit includes an implementation framework, which addresses strategies and practices for successfully gaining business and IT buy-in, and includes descriptions of key architecture processes and roles.

6. Q. How can you translate conceptual architecture into reality?

    A. The Toolkit includes a step-by-step approach to translating architecture into manageable projects—how to identify, select, and downsize architecture projects.

7. Q. What is the role of the architect?

    A. The Toolkit includes descriptions of key architecture roles.

8. Q. How can you measure/cost justify architecture?

    A. The Toolkit addresses financial considerations and measurement development.

Acknowledgments

For all their help in getting this book birthed, I want to thank the staff at Prentice-Hall, especially the wonderful, persistent Harris Kern, Mayra Muniz, and Greg Doench. I also want to thank the folks at TIPS—Lynanne Fowle, Robert Kern, and Ariel Tuplano for all their help.

I thank and salute my partners in crime—MaryAnne Reuther, Jim Dixon, and Janet Wagner—for their support.

I am grateful to my friends and colleagues—especially Rae Scott and Ros Cannell—and Bob Paskus, Doug Seale, Mark Madaus, Mindy Macey, Iris Fliegelman, and the gang at AT&T.

I would like to remember Bernie Boar—a colleague and friend.

And last, but not least, I thank my family for their enduring support—Mom, Paul, Cathy, Liz, and Denise—and as always, this is for Chris, Jenny, and dad.

About The Author

Jane Carbone is a co-founder of and partner at infomajic. She has over 25 years of experience in information technology working with network provisioning, finance, regulatory, customer sales and service, billing, and financial and credit applications. Ms. Carbone has developed and used the infomajic enterprise information architecture methodology to conduct and develop architecture assessments, enterprise and data architectures, IT strategies, data models, organization designs, and implementation project plans for financial services companies, IT HR and telecomm firms, and the public library.

Prior to forming infomajic, Ms. Carbone was the Director of Information Architecture Services at Datanomics, Inc., where she formed an architecture consulting practice. Prior to that, Ms. Carbone was with AT&T, where she was responsible for enterprise architecture for the consumer business unit. She was also responsible for developing and implementing the client/server architecture for AT&T American Transtech (now a unit of Convergys Corporation). Ms. Carbone was a member of the Gartner Group's Client/Server Best Practices Group. Working together with Gartner analysts, the group created research notes on all aspects of client/server architecture.

Ms. Carbone's experience also includes teaching analysis and data modeling, leading an enterprise data modeling team, developing and managing an enterprise-wide data stewardship program, managing HR and business planning for IT organization, managing data and voice network operations, and IT organization and job design. She has designed and developed software, and developed and taught programming and design courses.

Ms. Carbone delivers three-day architecture workshops for clients and one-day seminars for METAGroup/DCI Enterprise Architectures conferences. Her architecture seminars are available online through DCI. She has spoken on architecture at other DCI and DAMA conferences and is a past board member of DAMA-NJ. Her articles have been published in DMDirect, the TDAN Newsletter, and on *eacommunity.com*.

Ms. Carbone has a B.A. in English Literature and Language and an M.S. in Library and Information Science.

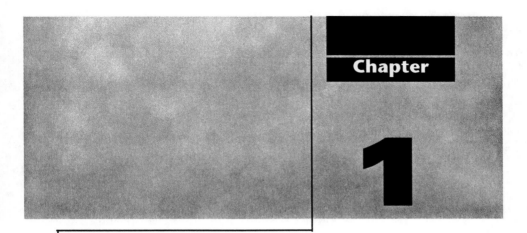

Introduction

The Role of IT Planning

If information is "gold," and I had staked my fortune (or my company) on mining it, I fervently hope that I would have started with a plan on how to go about it. As an acquaintance once said, "We don't plan to fail, we fail to plan." Yet, after so many years in IT, I have seen—and been part of—many organizations that fail to plan. They may believe it is too time-consuming or too expensive. Proceeding with large, complex, and often mission-critical IT initiatives without prior planning, however, often leads to disastrous outcomes.

I have recently been reminded of how apt the comparison between IT architecture and building a house is. I learned again that what you plan is more likely to happen, that what you include in the plan is most likely to be executed, and that what you omit will likely not see the light of day.

1

Here are some examples of what really happens when there is little or no IT planning, poor IT planning, or unintegrated IT planning.

- A four-year operational scheduling project did not make it into production because the technology plan was never synched up with the business and architecture plans. The result: By the time the technology was fixed, the business function was drastically downsized, and the new application was overkill.

- A critical five-year enterprise database project was still struggling for acceptance because the project leadership focused almost entirely on new technology rather than trying to satisfy primary urgent business needs. The result: Funding was cut.

- A major multiyear billing system overhaul began coding before the architecture was built and the platform selected. The result: The project faces ongoing delays.

- An extremely complex three-year enterprise sales and ordering system rewrite became mired in conflict. An overly intricate technical design was completed and building began without a negotiated agreement with interfacing functions and systems. The result: The project was cancelled.

Architecture is *not* a silver bullet. IT implementations, however, stand a much better chance for success when:

- Business is involved in IT planning, and the business objectives are clear to IT;
- Diverse business needs and respective IT solutions resulting from business changes (e.g., consolidations, acquisitions, resizing) are recognized;
- Conflicting goals of internal organizations surface and major problems can be cooperatively resolved;
- IT plans capture and incorporate problem resolutions; and
- IT plans drive application and data store development and technology selection.

Four Mini Case Studies—Best (and Worst) Practices

If we believe that having an IT plan is necessary, then how do we best construct one? The following are actual profiles of attempts at building architectures. Perhaps you will identify with some of the ups and downs, successes and failures we describe here.

Case Study 1–1 was one of my earlier architecture experiences. You can probably tell that, while the business connection was great, the technology connection was absent—leading to some severe problems.

Case Study 1–2 was one of my favorite jobs. In this situation, almost everything worked well. Having the responsibility for all the related functions in one place led to tremendous benefit.

Case Study 1–3 was one of my most difficult "learning experiences." This tale might be subtitled "How Overkill Can Lead to Rejection." Of course, the lack of business participation was equally disastrous.

Case Study 1–4 is where it all came together for me. I had learned my lessons well and put all my experience to work. Ah, the sweet smell of success—or why an architect needs to focus, pay attention to politics (a personal Waterloo), and include supporting processes.

Update an aging mainframe infrastructure and outdated operational methods.

Organizational profile

- A customer service business unit with more than 30,000 employees
- A team of eight analysts/architects reporting to the business unit
- An IT staff of about sixty

Approach used

- The architecture team initiated quarterly meetings with a large (more than 100 people) business user forum
- The architects developed high-level current and target state business and architecture models, created prototypes, and reviewed them with the user forum
- The architects created very detailed function and data descriptions
- The technology selection was made by a separate organization

What worked

- The business users were very engaged in the process
- The substance and scope of proposed infrastructure changes was very clear in the models and prototypes, and the business users both understood and supported the changes

What did not work

- The function and data descriptions were so detailed that the architects were "married" to the development organization—there were not enough architects to also act as analysts and cover all the bases
- The selected technology did not support the architecture, causing multiyear delays

Migrate mission-critical application from mainframe to client/server architecture.

Organizational profile

- A customer service company of about 12,000 employees
- IT staff of 500
- A small, part-time architecture team reporting to IT

Approach used

- Business unit representatives—marketing and operations—participated in the modeling team
- The team created the IT business plan and developed high-level process, data, and technology models
- The architects used the modeling outputs to build a very detailed architecture framework, construct the architecture, create data and technology standards, and purchase hardware and software
- The architecture team arranged for supporting training and managed IT recruiting
- The IT organization established a team to manage standards and review compliance

What worked

- Business users could understand and buy into the process and data models
- Developers could work from the detailed architecture models and technical standards

Find a way to implement target architecture in a large business.

Organization profile

- A very large consumer telephony organization
- IT staff of more than 4000
- A cross-IT organization team of over twenty architects

Approach used

- The IT leadership represented the business needs
- The architects developed a rigorous, detailed framework and content, including a set of very complex graphical models
- The architects built a detailed three-year implementation roadmap with a list of almost 100 megaprojects

What worked

- The plan was very integrated and complete
- The architects gained a tremendous breadth of cross-enterprise knowledge, and the knowledge was reusable

What did not work

- The business leadership did not understand the architecture
- The IT leadership found the scope of the architecture threatening and an invasion of "turf"
- The scope was self-defeating—too many projects

Try again to find a way to implement target
architecture in a large business.

Organization profile

- The same very large consumer telephony organization
- IT staff of about 4000
- Fewer members (seven) of the same cross-IT architecture team

Approach used

- The architects connected with the business by participating in the formal business planning and funding process
- The architects developed a greatly simplified framework
- The architects developed high-level models for the business leaders and decomposed the models for developers
- The architects selected the top ten projects to propose and developed business metrics for each
- The architects developed and proposed a compliance process
- The basic architecture was unchanged, but significant time and energy were devoted to presenting key components of the architecture in a meaningful way to the business and IT leadership

What worked

- The business leadership understood the plan
- The IT leadership supported the plan
- They all liked the slides and the metrics
- The "top ten" was feasible
- The project managers and developers understood the architecture
- The team of architects "morphed" into an architecture council that met regularly to review development projects for architecture compliance
- Linkage to the business planning/funding process was established and maintained

What did not work
- It took time for the compliance process to take root and become more formalized

Introducing the Enterprise Architecture Toolkit

These scenarios both highlight common mistakes and reinforce the need for an IT planning methodology *that works*. Necessity being the mother of invention, I was forced to invent one. It was driven by my belief that the purpose of enterprise architecture is to align the IT infrastructure with the organization in a way that best promotes the organization's goals, while maximizing the benefit of IT dollars spent. I think this applies to any organization investing in IT. For us, there were no architecture "cookbooks," but rather trial and error, skilled and talented people, and challenging assignments that brought about this birth.

I would like to call the methodology we developed, *Eight Easy Steps to Architecture Success*, but since I am (basically) truthful, I have to admit that it is really more simple and necessary than easy. Instead, we called our methodology the *Enterprise Architecture Toolkit*, and it is based on what we have learned in the field.

- Business involvement is a must—it is ideal to have a small business team with a big communications channel.
- While a highly structured approach to architecture may be a good fit for a small, highly structured organization, a simpler, "smaller is better" approach to architecture has advantages when:
  - The business is very large or complex;
  - Knowledge of the business is spread out or isolated in "stovepipes;" and
  - The architects have a narrow scope, narrow architecture experience, or are understaffed, and the organization has limited time/patience/resources/affection for IT planning.
- The scope of architecture needs to be expressed in easily understood frameworks and standard outputs.
- The architects must translate the outputs to key implementation projects with business metrics.
- The data, function, technology, people, process, and financial planning need to be closely linked.
- The architecture process needs to include some form of IT governance to guide development.
- A smaller (e.g., five to eight people) rather than larger architecture team works best. The architects require broad

business knowledge and deep IT experience to develop the necessary outputs.

- The architects must also be able to develop very high-level conceptual outputs to gain support and communicate the architecture across organizations.

Getting Started

So, how can architects begin to achieve this utopia? The information in this book is intended to provide practical help for architects to take these not-so-easy steps. To create and implement a truly achievable plan for IT, the architecture needs to address everything from the key business drivers to overcoming likely resistance. Before you become discouraged, let us introduce a solution—one we know works.

Our solution is a simplified set of methods and practices that:

- Was developed based on lessons learned/best practices;
- Includes three frameworks—business, architecture, and implementation frameworks; and
- Is very practical—it meets the business challenges of tight timeframes, resource constraints, and ongoing course corrections.

Let us begin with some of the basic definitions we use. The plan for IT can also be called an "enterprise architecture."

- "Enterprise" means all parts of the company, business unit, agency, or organization. In this book, these terms are used interchangeably.
- "Architecture" means the set of plans that describe how all parts of the IT infrastructure need to behave to support the enterprise needs and goals. It includes all the data required to run the enterprise and the functions, technology, and people that create, access, use, or transform that data into information—and ultimately, knowledge for the business.

Components of an Enterprise Architecture

For better or worse, enterprise architecture requires us to set a realistic scope for architecture within a broader-than-technical perspective. Figure 1–1 shows the scope of outputs we have found must be addressed for architecture to succeed. We call the set of outputs and the methods used to create them the *Enterprise Architecture Toolkit* (herein after referred to as "Toolkit").

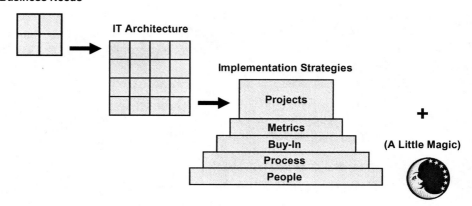

Figure 1–1   infomajic Enterprise Architecture Toolkit.

The Toolkit includes three frameworks.

Business Framework

The Business Framework provides a roadmap for collecting and analyzing key knowledge about the enterprise that will *drive* architecture.

IT Framework

The IT Framework provides a roadmap for creating the outputs of IT architecture *and their relationships* that will enable business goals.[1]

---

1. While the business and implementation frameworks are of our own creation, we believe the IT framework to be based on a framework from CSC/Index Technologies, but could find no reference after an extensive search.

Implementation Framework

Finally, the Toolkit includes a set of implementation strategies. These include best practices for addressing key areas that enable the *actualization* of the architecture.

A Comparison of the Toolkit and the Zachman Framework

John Zachman is truly the "Father of Enterprise Architecture." The framework he has developed has motivated hundreds—probably thousands—of IT planners to evaluate and consider what is really necessary to create an IT plan and why it is such an important undertaking. Because we are asked in almost every presentation and workshop how our Toolkit compares with the Zachman Framework for Enterprise Architecture,[2] we will try to address that question here. The Toolkit frameworks are both consistent with and diverge from the Zachman Framework.

The Toolkit's Business Framework is roughly aligned with the "cells" in the Objectives/Scope row of the Zachman Framework—that is, the Toolkit addresses the Data, Function, Network/Technology, People, Time, and Motivation cells. What the Toolkit adds are guidelines for collecting this data and some methods for how to capture the data in a form that can be translated to architecture outputs. In the Toolkit, the ability to integrate outputs within and across frameworks is a key concept. In fact, it is a prime driver for many of the methods. And because we have found the business connection to be so vital, we wanted to emphasize its importance by capturing the business needs in a separate framework.

The Toolkit's Architecture Framework is roughly aligned with the Business Model (Conceptual) and Systems Model (Logical) rows of the Zachman Framework. The Toolkit begins to venture into the Technology Model (physical)—but only at the highest level—by assigning technology to the lowest-level architecture models and by developing technology inventory and standards. The scope of our approach is IT planning and strategy (the Planner, Owner, and Designer views in

---

[2.] The Zachman framework has been presented at countless IT conferences. My latest copy is from John Zachman's presentation "You Can't 'Cost Justify' Architecture," which was delivered at the DAMA International Symposium in San Antonio, Texas, on April 28, 2002.

Zachman), and does not include analysis and design (in Zachman, the Builder and Subcontractor views), except to illustrate where that line is crossed and some examples of how to cross it.

In addition, the Toolkit includes a Framework for Implementation. We have learned (the hard way!) that unless the IT plan includes certain project-, process-, and people-focused plans and activities, even the best architecture may never begin to be realized.

Critical Success Factors

In case the frameworks figure was not worth a thousand words, the following are what we have learned are the critical success factors for IT architecture:

- A clear understanding of where the business is going versus where it is
- An architecture scope that covers all the bases in the most simple, effective ways
- The translation of the architecture to a small set of well-scoped, business-oriented projects
- The development and tracking of metrics for each project
- The packaging or marketing of the architecture
- Processes that support the architecture and the architects

And, of course, it does not hurt to have boundless enthusiasm and remarkable perseverance. I once had a boss who wrote on my performance appraisal "She is very stubborn." This is the kind of perseverance I mean.

A Word about Integration

The Toolkit defines all the pieces of an architecture. What may not be apparent from the picture is that each output created using our three frameworks is not created independently—outputs are related to each otherr. In this book, we will describe not only how to construct an IT plan, but also how to insure that it is integrated. We will address integration from several points of view: integration of the architecture with the business, integration across the IT framework architecture outputs, and integration of the architecture with the organization. Figure 1–2 illustrates the process flow behind the Toolkit and describes the implicit integration across framework outputs.

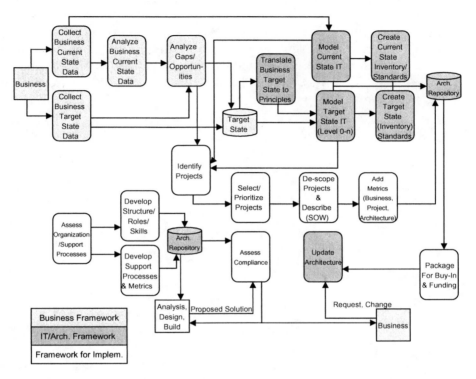

Figure 1–2 Toolkit process flow.

How This Book Is Organized

The purpose of our Toolkit is to provide a proven, simplified set of methods for constructing enterprise architecture within the real-life constraints of tight timeframes, limited resources, and ongoing business course corrections (a.k.a. nonstop change). The tension between business realities and the desire to do a perfect job can be unbearable. Since the business constraints are a given, the Toolkit provides a way to deliver "good enough" architecture.

Because the Toolkit is a set of practices for creating architecture outputs, the remaining chapters of the book each address a Toolkit framework output. For each output there are definitions, guidelines, and examples. The "Toolkit dictionary" definitions are included because commonly used terms may have specific meaning in the Toolkit. The guidelines are the "meat," or the methods for how to construct the component. The examples are based on a compendium of real work experiences, disguised to "protect the guilty." For each architecture output there is a suggested exercise. If you create the outputs described in the exercises, you will have a working draft of enterprise architecture for your organization.

The Toolkit Business Framework: Connecting Architecture to the Business

The Business Framework

In my experience, the two "cardinal sins" of architecture are an overly complex, technocentric view of the world and a lack of clear business focus. As the examples in Chapter 1 demonstrate, IT projects that begin without a genuine understanding of the business needs and without business involvement often fail. Doing a high-level, up-front review of where the business is now and where it wants to be in the future is so critical that the Toolkit specifically includes a framework designed for collecting and analyzing key enterprise business information.

A basic version of the business framework is shown in Figure 2–1.

15

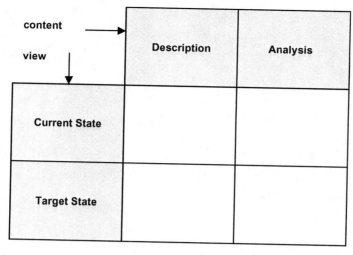

	Description	Analysis
Current State		
Target State		

content → view ↓

Figure 2–1   The EA Toolkit business framework.

Here are some business framework fundamentals and Toolkit definitions for the business framework constructs.

- The rows describe the business view—a snapshot of where the business is at a point in time. The most important views are *current state* and *target state*, but other views can be included (e.g., one-year view). The *Business Current State* describes how the enterprise is operating today—"what is." The *Business Target State* describes how the enterprise wants to operate in the future—"what will be."

- The columns describe the business content outputs—data to be captured and addressed in IT architecture.

The purpose of the business framework is to provide a vehicle for identifying a basic, minimum set of information about the business that ought to drive architecture. While there is a truckload of information you could collect, the framework identifies what is necessary to collect. While it could take months to collect information about the business, we can effectively shorten the collection time by narrowing the focus. In fact, if it takes more than a few weeks to collect the business framework information, it may indicate a lack of support or ineffective participation.

The business framework provides structure around what information is to be collected. Its use results in a set of outputs specifically designed to be input into the work done using the IT framework (traditional architecture). This helps us to achieve the fundamental integration of business needs and opportunities in the IT plans.

Describing the Business Current State—Collecting Key Facts

"Just the facts, ma'am..." Sgt. Joe Friday, Dragnet

Here are some approaches we have found to be helpful in describing the current state of the enterprise. While there is much more information you could collect about any organization, you can limit your data collection to a few essentials. Use one, or better still, a combination of these approaches, to identify and record information that captures the current focus and bottom line concerns of the business. You should not expect to spend more than a few weeks constructing the business current state. If you have not collected most of the information below in the first couple of weeks, then your sources may be unclear about organizational goals, or you may need to get stronger management support for your data collection.

The following are my top priorities when describing the current state.

1. Collect the most visible and most accepted business strategy documents that capture the business purpose (e.g., Mission/Goals Statements, Strategic and Operational Business Plans, Key Business Initiatives/Major Programs).

2. Interview the organization's leaders to ask and record what potential business sponsors and key opinion leaders have to say about what is right and wrong with the business. Construct open-ended questions (e.g., "What are your goals?" "What works well today?" "What would you change?").

3. Recognize and account for "history" or "culture" and significant changes in business direction (e.g., e-Business; recent or planned mergers, acquisitions, or consolidations; deregulation; new ventures or products; or new technology).

4. Identify key business drivers that describe the major themes or motivational forces that impact the behavior of the organization (e.g., "buy or be bought").

5. Identify key constraints (e.g., regulatory, legislative, or shareholder considerations over which the organization has little or no control).

6. Gather "basic information" that creates a portrait of the organization. The "Five Ws" provide a good start.
    - *What* What does the organization do—its purpose, its reason for being (e.g., "sell widgets")
    - *When* Key events or historical change that has or will have an impact on how the organization operates or will need to operate—major turning points
    - *How* In what ways does the organization conduct business (e.g., online research, retail sales centers)
    - *Who* The organization, its customers, suppliers, partners
    - *Why* Problems causing a rethinking or change in strategies and business drivers—why is this [situation] not working? Why do we need to do something different?

7. Here are some other suggestions. Capture:
    - Company size in annual revenue, expenses, and number of employees;
    - Number and types of customers;
    - Locations served and serving ;
    - List of products and services, and quantity sold;
    - High-level organizational structure and/or process flow;
    - Sales channels;
    - Key suppliers/vendors;
    - Key reports or indices;
    - Current technology; and
    - External interfaces (e.g., government agency).

We often use a questionnaire and interviews to collect the data in items 2 through 7. The most-repeated responses help in spotting recurring themes and severe problems. The groups we prefer to interview include high-ranking business leaders, key opinion leaders in the business, and IT leaders, including the CIO. A sample questionnaire can be found in Appendix A. Appendix A lists associated documents we request from interviewees and architects to provide additional data. You may also want to get management support to set up a steering committee or a team of key organizational stakeholders to provide initial business input and direction, and to review and provide ongoing feedback to the architecture team.

Here is an example of applying these guidelines. We constructed a fictitious company (CDCo, and its acquisition, Bookseller) to illustrate how to construct Toolkit outputs. We use this example company throughout the book. This will help to illustrate the relationships between outputs.

These are the 5 Ws (*basic information*, item 6 above) we collected from the annual report and interviews with key opinion leaders at CDCo and Bookseller. You may recognize some of the strengths and weaknesses attributed to CDCo in your own enterprise.

CDCo, Inc. is a stable, publicly held retail music chain that sells CDs and DVDs and still maintains an inventory of records, tapes, posters, and sheet music for collectors. CDCo sold almost 300 million items in 1999, with revenues of close to $2.5 billion.

In December 1999 the board of CDCo voted to expand into the book/magazine product line and acquired Bookseller, Inc. Currently, CDCo interacts with customers via the following:

- 427 retail outlets in 49 states and 3 international sites
- A profitable, medium-sized call center (1-800-CALL4CD)

CDCo just set up a very simple website to address competition from e-tailers and free downloads, and is still trying to get the connections with its back office (legacy) functions working. As a result, customer complaints have increased about 30 percent. Currently, there is no automated support for integrating publications and special promotions into its Web offerings, as customers have requested, but CDCo wants very much to leverage the Web as a sales channel.

CDCo has information about millions of customers from its CDClub card applications—the CDClub card promotes repeat sales by offering discounts to registered customers. Applications are kept in individual (Access) files in retail outlets and in a central (Oracle) database for card applications received via the call center. It is difficult to identify current club members because some have applied for cards both at a store and over the phone and have not always provided consistent responses to the application. CDCo wants to understand and better use customer demographics and purchase history information to leverage existing customer sales.

CDCo recently outsourced its inventory/distribution to an external supplier and is still working through the logistics around fulfilling and confirming orders via the vendor. New processes are causing delays and mistakes.

CDCo has an employee base of 3,898 full- and part-time employees who are retail and call center sales agents and managers, music buyers, IT staff, and administrative support. The Web focus is so important to marketing that the organization created a new Web development group of five employees. This group reports to sales and is organizationally separate from the current IT staff.

Bookseller had been a privately held, family-run company that sold a broad spectrum of books, magazines, and newspapers. In 1999, Bookseller earned $1.2 billion in revenue on sales of 100 million publications.

Bookseller's growth rate has been accelerating because of very successful website sales. The success is straining the current infrastructure. Through its website book club, Bookseller has begun to track customers. Bookseller also interacts with customers via 229 retail outlets in 40 states.

Bookseller manages its own inventory/distribution with three super-warehouses.

The Bookseller employee base consists of 2,493 employees in sales, management, buying, warehousing/distribution, IT, and administrative support.

Bookseller spending on manual processes—especially customer service—in support of Web sales is spiraling up. Bookseller hopes to reduce expenses through improved processes and technology.

Here is one of CDCo's most broadly distributed documents (item 1 above)—the "CDCo Statement of Goals"—which captures key business drivers:

If you have a one-page set of goals or key initiatives for your organization, it can provide current state information because these usually identify problems the organization plans to overcome. In the example above, we can tell that CDCo currently does not know enough about its customers to enable better marketing, retention, and customer satisfaction, and that CDCo believes it is not flexible enough in its ability to respond to change.

Suggested Exercise

At this point, you may want to stop and collect basic current state information about your enterprise.

Another Approach to Describing the Current State

One of the other approaches we use for describing both the current and target states is to develop a process flow for either state of the business, by translating current or future processes and information into functions and information flow. At this point in the process, it is usually sufficient to keep any diagrams very simple, since their purpose is to capture major problems or changes. We will talk about process flows soon.

Next, we will look at some techniques for how to analyze the data you have collected.

The Toolkit Business Framework: Analyzing the Business Current State

I feel more comfortable when the "diagnosis" precedes the "prescription."

Time and again, we have been part of or worked with IT organizations that, in their desire to put an architecture in place, gloss over or entirely skip the vital steps that tie the architecture to the business. This "putting the cart before the horse" often results in missed or incorrect IT targets. So do not give in to those urges to select the new platform before understanding the current state of the business. This chapter provides some approaches for understanding how the enterprise is operating today.

Using Assessment Indicators

We begin by applying *Assessment Indicators*—factors used to analyze the business current state data collected in Chapter 2. Much like a thermometer, they provide a way to gauge the health or temperature of the business and to identify key symptoms or problems.

Here are guidelines for analyzing the business current state using assessment indicators. Review the data you collected in Chapter 2 and respond to the following key indicators to analyze the data. Document your conclusions.

- *Stress Points/Risks*   Identify and list significant "stress points" or risks in the enterprise. These are longer-term major factors that may cause extreme change and require a proactive stance, e.g., significant decline, unexpected growth. What are the worries/possible downsides of the current business plan?

- *Strengths and Weaknesses*   Analyze and list the strengths and weaknesses of the enterprise, e.g., employee loyalty, low turnover. These are usually characteristics for which the organization is known or recognized.

- *Challenges*   Extract the major challenges the enterprise faces. A challenge is a shorter-term situation the organization is trying to accommodate (often reactively), e.g., competition from e-tailors. You can usually recognize a challenge by the fact that several different groups are working to address it.

- *Environmental Factors*   List the major external environmental factors that impact the enterprise. These are forces outside of the control of the enterprise that require response, e.g., new legislation, deregulation.

- *Growth/Cost Containment Opportunities*   Extract potential growth and cost containment opportunities available to the enterprise. These represent desired positive outcomes, e.g., "Combining book and CD offers with free gifts could enhance revenue." You can sometimes recognize a potential growth/cost savings opportunity by the fact that a new "buzzword" has cropped up, and everyone wants to be associated with it.

For example, when we applied Assessment Indicators to the current state description of CDCo, here is some of what we found.

- *Stress Point/Risk*   Revenue growth is beginning to erode due to increased competition from online music retailers.
- *Weaknesses*   Customer needs and characteristics are changing. Bargain-oriented, e-savvy customers want to make unique combinations of purchases and payments via their channel of choice and receive rewards. CDCo has no on-line/automatic bill payment capability, nor the ability to package custom offers of books and music with purchasing incentives.
- *Challenges*   Problems with the accuracy and speed of delivery of products by the new outsource vendor for inventory/shipping is causing customer complaints. Also, Customer Service can't keep up with customer complaints.
- *Environmental Factor*   The outcome of legislation regulating the downloading of free music is unclear.
- *Growth/cost containment opportunity*   Service offerings can expand through the acquisition of Bookseller. Also, valuable customer information is available through club membership applications. Additionally, there are two separate IT groups, plus a CDCo Web team, each providing redundant infrastructure and using incompatible tools, development life cycle methodologies and data. Finally, the company wants to increase the growth rate and revenue from music sales and maintain the growth rate in publications.

For Bookseller we also identified several indicators.

- *Stress Points/Risks*   Key customer information is beginning to become available through the Bookseller online club and some customer data is not automated or not easily accessible. In fact, it is very difficult to identify who the customers are. Also, some sales results information is automated, but there are separate reports from Web site and retail stores, so the answer to "Are we making a profit?" is not readily apparent or reliable.
- *Weakness*   Employee loyalty is extremely high, but employees rely heavily on relationships versus processes.
- *Challenge*   The current processes and systems are frantically trying to keep up with business changes and increased Web sales volume. Many loyal employees are devising individual means to

maintain customer satisfaction. It's difficult to tell what solutions are working.

- *Growth/cost containment opportunity*   The web site is very popular and web sales are increasing. Also, as a result of reliance on people, relationships and manual intervention, overhead expenses seem to be higher than necessary.

Environmental Scan

Another way to approach analyzing the current state is to perform an *environmental scan*. An environmental scan—the review of industry-specific research, trade associations, conferences, and publications to detect trends that affect your organization—can provide good information for assessing how the current state of your organization stacks up against your industry or competitors. A scan may highlight a problem in the current state that might have gone otherwise undetected.

For CDCo, an environmental scan surfaced changes in potential customer behavior that could impact the company. Here is an excerpt of the scan:

By the numbers

How Americans are using household communications and computing technology now available to them:

- 45 percent of all Americans use cellular or wireless phones
- 43 percent use computers
- 37 percent use email
- 31 percent use the Internet for more than just email
- 25 percent use fax machines
- 12 percent bank online
- 11 percent shop online
- 23 percent use none of the above

(From *The Courier News*, May 8, 2000, paraphrasing a survey conducted by *Wired* magazine)

Nearly half of U.S. Internet users have purchased a product or service online. The most popular item purchased is books—42 percent have bought them online—compared to 38 percent for music purchases and 29 percent for software.

(Source: ACNielson, *EAI Journal*, June 6, 2000)

Suggested Exercise

At this point, you may want to stop and use one or more of the approaches we have just described to analyze the current state information you collected about your enterprise.

Using Process Flows

Before we leave the current business state, we have one more suggestion. We brought up process flows at the end of Chapter 2. If you have the resources or existing documents, you might also construct a *current business flow*, containing major processes, sequences, and critical information. We bring up process flows here because of the following.

- A good way to collect information and pin-point problems during an interview is to:
  - Ask questions about how/if major processes are connected/disconnected, and
  - Capture responses in a flow diagram.
- Most serious business problems are the result of broken processes.
- A process flow can help eliminate the capture of "noise" (relatively unimportant areas of focus for the architect).

We advocate the addition of this third approach to analyzing the business current state because it will help in the translation of business framework outputs to architecture outputs. This is especially true when you can take advantage of interviewees to review your drafts or to provide commentary on existing flow documents (e.g., "This is a bottleneck!"). Figure 3–1 is an example of the kind of simple business process flow we construct, and we will discuss more about business flows in coming chapters.

Next we will look at some techniques for how to collect the data about the target state of the business.

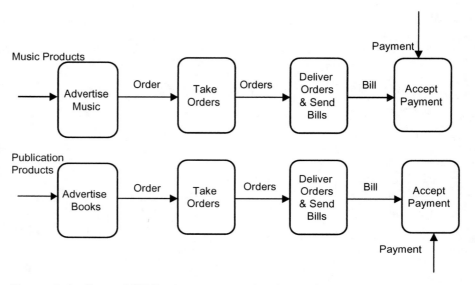

Figure 3–1   Part of CDCo current state business flow.

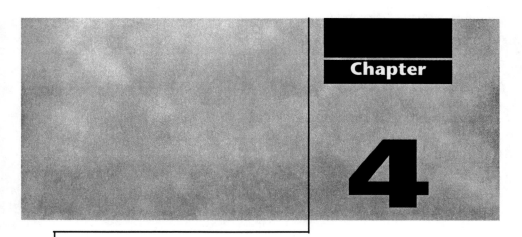

The Toolkit Business Framework: Constructing the Business Target State

"Begin with the end in mind..." (standard quality improvement advice)

Now that we have developed a baseline description of where the business is today, we will focus on describing where the business wants to go. The *business target state* describes the positive characteristics of the desired future state of the business—"what will be." In one sense, the target state describes how the business will operate if current state problems are solved. In another sense, the target state embodies the achievement of mission and goals. This chapter describes guidelines for approaching the construction of the enterprise target state description from both perspectives.

Much of the information you collected when you documented the business current state will be helpful in describing the business target state. And even though the target state may seem obvious, try not to rush to judgment or jump right to conclusions. There are a couple of approaches we use to systematically define the target state and begin to build linkages that will flow right through to implementation.

Using Assessment Indicators

The first approach requires that you construct *positive statements* to broadly describe the target state by *reversing* the responses to the current business state analysis. Describe how the business would behave if:

- Stress points were relaxed/risks mitigated;
- Weaknesses were addressed and strengths fortified;
- Challenges were resolved;
- Environment changes were accounted for; and
- Growth/cost containment opportunities were leveraged.

For example, a student asked me how to reverse a current state stress when the stressor was a fact of the business. In this situation, the geographic disbursement of business units caused ongoing communications problems, which negatively impacted project implementations. I suggested that, because it was not reasonable to ask the business to move all its employees to one location, it would be worthwhile to address the result of the disbursement, which was poor communications. In this case, I suggested that a target state description might be: "New processes (or methods, tools, etc.) improve cross-business unit communication, thereby supporting project implementation."

The following is how we described the CDCo Target Business State.

- *Stress Points/Risks* Stress points were relaxed/risks mitigated.
  - Revenue is growing due to an enhanced website.
- *Weakness* Weaknesses were addressed and strengths fortified.
  - CDCo has an easy-to-use, online, and automatic bill payment capability.
  - CDCo can easily package offers of books, music, and incentives that buyers want.

- *Challenge*   Challenges were resolved.
  - New b2b e-commerce exchange has improved the accuracy of inventory/shipping and reduced the number of customer complaints.
  - A new trouble management process facilitates customer service (in this example, we include theoretical technology—this may come directly from an officer's statement).
- *Environment change*   Environment changes were accounted for.
  - The strategy for competing with the downloading of free music is in place and addresses potential regulatory outcomes.
- *Growth/cost containment opportunity*   Growth opportunities were leveraged.
  - Service offerings have expanded through the acquisition of Bookseller
  - The consolidated website enables complex sales and is supported by backend systems and processes.
  - An integrated IT team enables business integration.
  - Customer club card information is continually used to effectively target new offers.

A student once asked how to use this approach when the current state *problem* was a given (e.g., Challenge: Remote office locations tend to create and use their own systems [processes, etc.] causing duplication). In this situation, it is very unlikely that the management of the remote locations will be centralized, so I would recommend focusing on the result of the problem, which is duplication. In this example, a target state reversal would address the duplication (e.g., all locations will use common systems, processes, etc.).

Using Process Flows

The second approach is based on the enterprise vision for the future. This approach allows you to describe the target state in more depth.

Seek out information and documents that allow you to answer the following questions. In the *ideal* future...

1. How will customers and suppliers interact with the enterprise? If bottlenecks or gaps have been identified in the current state, we want to examine how to address them in the target state (e.g., "Suppliers will accept our orders electronically and deliver directly to the customer's address.").

2. What would the future high-level business function flow look like? We recommend the construction of very simple flows—major business functions and critical data flows—for the target state. Of course, if we created a current state process flow, we would have a head start on the construction of a target state flow. Since current state flows often highlight severe problems—redundant or disconnected processes—some areas that need to be addressed in the target state flow are often readily apparent. Figure 4–1 illustrates a basic target business function flow for CDCo.

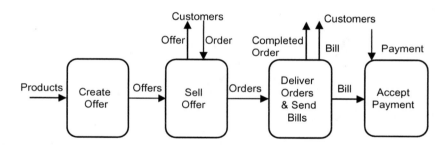

Figure 4–1 Sample target state business flow.

3. What key business information will flow through the process? Many key sets of information—especially missing or unreliable information—were probably identified in the current state analysis. The target information—complete, repaired, or accurate information—should be added to the target state process flow (e.g., combined offers, customer sales profiles).

4. What critical people plans and skills will be in place? If current state analysis picks up people problems (e.g., skill deficits, performance deficiencies) or goals have been defined for employees, this is the place to begin to capture how employees

will operate in the future (e.g., "All sales employees have web skills;" "There is a single, cross-trained IT organization.").

5. What critical support processes and structures will be in place? If manual intervention or duplicate processes have been identified in the current state, then the target state description should address these concerns (e.g.,"The new skills assessment process is used by all managers;" "Performance incentives maintain employee loyalty").

6. What key capabilities will enable the desired state? Here we want to identify functionality that is completely missing in the current state and has been identified by a business leader or industry trend as being highly desirable in the future (e.g., "We have the capability for a customer with a service problem to reach a live agent from the website.").

Here is how we used the second approach with CDCo (by item number from the list above).

1. Interactions with customers and suppliers?
   - Customers: "Customers can access a single, full-service website with ordering and payment options to maximize e-business."
   - Suppliers: "Vendors become partners so orders and shipments are on time and highly accurate (electronic ordering capability?)."

3. Process and information flow?
   - "Sales are counted uniformly, and tracked from order through delivery, and are collected for quick and easy marketing analysis."
   - "Customer characteristics, preferences, and responses are collected from targeting through problem resolution, improving customer satisfaction, targeting, sales, and revenue." Figure 4–2 illustrates the target state information for CDCo.

4. Critical people, plans, and processes?
   - People: "All sales people are certified in new sales skills training, which includes up-to-date technology training."
   - Compensation process: "Most employees receive new annual bonuses by qualifying for superior sales performance evaluation."

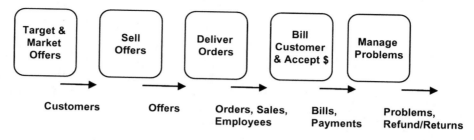

Figure 4–2   Part of CDCo target business function/information flow.

5. Key enabling capabilities?

  - "There are Customer Relationship Management (CRM) strategies/tools in place that enable *seamless* communication, regardless of channel, when CDCo interacts with customers."

  - "The new combined Web offer capability allows for near real-time additions and changes to services."

Digging Down

Another approach is to take a goals or initiatives document and decompose it. For example, when we investigated "Leverage technology" from the CDCo Statement of Goals, we found it really meant that:

- CDCo wants to deploy a standard platform for its call center agents to facilitate change and training;

- CDCo business leaders believe too much is spent on new technology before current technology is fully utilized; and

- Some leaders believe that Bookseller has technology CDCo could use to its advantage.

By the time we have collected, documented, and organized this information—and process flows encourage the organization of the information—we will have a fairly succinct picture of where the enterprise desires to be. Again, we are talking about days versus weeks of work, and pages versus volumes of outputs.

Suggested Exercise

At this point, you may want to stop and use one or more of the approaches we have just described to begin to draft a target state picture of your enterprise.

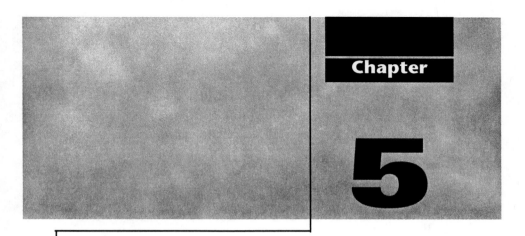

The Toolkit Business Framework: Analyzing the Target State— Identifying Gaps and Opportunities

What is wrong with this picture?

In this chapter we will look at the practices we use to explicitly compare the current and target business states. You should resist the temptation to bypass this step. While it may be obvious by this time what the differences between the current and target states are, formally performing (and documenting) this step not only provides an audit trail for architecture, but is crucial for the accurate translation of business needs into infrastructure plans. The comparison of the current state to the target state forms the bridge to architecture, providing direction and focus for what the architects need to address. Later chapters describe how this translation takes place.

Analyze the Target State

Analyzing the target state refers to the extraction of significant business opportunities and/or gaps to be addressed by IT architecture. What follows are guidelines for extracting those gaps and opportunities. The guidelines provide a straightforward approach to analyzing the target state. And of course, this work relies on the work done in earlier steps. This is part of the integration across the "cells" that results from using the business framework.

First Approach

In the first approach we compare significant stress points, strengths/weaknesses, challenges, environmental factors, and growth opportunities between the current state description and the target state description. For example, compare the following.

- *Current* Customers want to make purchases and payments via their channel of choice, and CDCo has no online or automatic bill-payment capability.
- *Target* Customers can access a single, full-service website with ordering and payment options.

We then *extract the opportunity*. The opportunity needs to describe an action or actions that can be taken to mitigate the difference between current and target states, so think verb-noun (e.g., develop online and/or automatic bill payment capability).

This following is a sample of potential opportunities we identified for CDCo using this method.

- Stress Point
  - *Current* CDCo just set up a very simple website to address competition from e-tailors. Revenue growth is eroding due to increased competition from online music retailers.
  - *Target* Customers and sales agents can access a single, full-service website with ordering and payment options to maximize e-business.

- *Opportunity* Consolidate websites. Design and implement new payment options.

- Environmental Change
  - *Current* The outcome of legislation regulating the downloading of free music is unclear.
  - *Target* The strategy for competing with the downloading of free music is in place and addresses potential regulatory outcomes (in this case, the outcome of legislation regulating the downloading of free music is still unclear).
  - *Opportunity* Develop strategies for competing with free music that complies with potential regulation.

- Growth/Cost Containment Opportunity
  - *Current* Service offerings can expand through the acquisition of Bookseller.
  - *Target* Customers can order any combination of products and pay online.
  - *Opportunity* Develop combo offers of book/music products. Make offers available online. Design and implement new payment options.

Second Approach

Next we examine a somewhat more complex approach to analyzing the target business state, but one that will simplify the translation to infrastructure planning. This is true because using this approach tends to result in less general, more specific opportunities for action, especially when analyzing flows.

1. Compare the current and target states.

Compare the roles of customers and suppliers, key functions and information flow, key capabilities, people plans, and supporting processes in the current state versus the target state using the following example as a guide.

- *Current Key Information Flow* CDCo has information about millions of customers from its CDClub card applications. The

CDClub card promotes repeat sales by offering discounts to registered customers. Applications are kept in individual (Access) files in retail outlets and in a central (Oracle) database for card applications received via the call center. It is difficult to identify current club members because some have applied for cards both at a store and over the phone and have not always provided consistent responses to the application.

- *Target*   Complete and consistent knowledge of customer purchases and preferences improves marketing and sales.

2. List the differences.

These are potential gaps, as exhibited in the following example.

- *Gap*   Not all customer information is captured, consistently available, or complete.

3. Reverse gap to opportunity.

- *Opportunity*   Capture customer information consistently, and make it as complete as possible and easily available to marketing.

Using this approach, here are a few potential gaps we found for CDCo.

- Supplier Role
  - *Current*   Problems with the accuracy and speed of product delivery by the new outsource vendor for inventory/shipping is causing customer complaints.
  - *Target*   Vendor orders and shipments are on time and highly accurate.
  - *Gap*   Order delivery performance does not meet speed and accuracy requirements.
  - *Opportunity*   Improve delivery performance—investigate vendor inducements, investigate electronic ordering/eb2b-exchange, and investigate use of Bookseller inventory/ shipping functions.

- Key Function/Information Flow (see Figure 5–1)
  - *Current* CDCo wants to understand and better use customer buying information.
  - *Target* Customer characteristics, preferences, and responses are collected from targeting through problem resolution.
  - *Gap* Customer information collection does not support analysis.
  - *Opportunity* Improve collection of customer information.
- Key Enabling Capabilities
  - *Current* There is no way for customers on the Web to reach a live agent.
  - *Target* There are customer relationship management (CRM) strategies/tools in place that enable seamless communication, regardless of channel, when CDCo interacts with customers.
  - *Gap* There is a lack of strategies for flexible, seamless customer interaction across channels.
  - *Opportunity* The CDCo can develop CRM strategies, investigate CRM tools, investigate click-to-call, and investigate a common Web front end for agents and customers with chat capability.
- People Plans/Processes
  - *Current* There are two separate IT groups plus a CDCo Web team. Target: a single, cross-trained IT organization.
  - *Gap* There is a lack of consolidated, cross-trained IT organization.
  - *Opportunity* CDCo can evaluate organization design, develop plan to consolidate, integrate IT staff, and inventory current training by employee.

Suggested Exercise

See if you can come up with a list of target state gaps or opportunities.

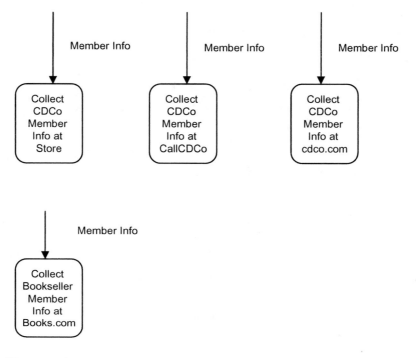

Figure 5–1 Pieces of CDCo/Bookseller current-state flow.

Integration

We have already mentioned integration several times. The ability to relate the output of one cell with the outputs of other cells is fundamental to the Toolkit. Here is an illustration of how business framework outputs are interrelated. Figure 5–2 follows one area of concern through the business framework cells.

Whether we use one or both of these approaches, by the time we're done we will have a working list of key areas to be addressed with architecture.

By following the process (Figure 5–3) we just described in the business framework, you will have created a set of target business opportunities to direct and drive the IT architecture effort. You will also have an audit trail—a set of linked outputs that describe how you

	Description	Analysis
Current State	<u>Key Facts</u> "(*CDCo*)...has no mechanized way to integrate publications, special promotions and combined offerings into its web catalog, and cannot accept on-line payments."	<u>Assessment Indicators Result</u> Growth Opportunity "Combining book, CD and promotional offers could enhance revenue."
Desired "Target" State	<u>Reverse Assessment Indicator</u> "Customers can order any combination of products and pay on-line".	<u>Target Opportunities</u> "Sell Combo Offers that include music, books, gifts and/ or new products." "Accept on-line and/or automatic bill payment."

Figure 5–2 Putting it together.

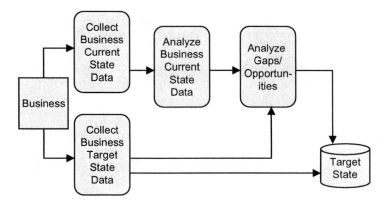

Figure 5–3 Toolkit process flow—business framework.

arrived at this destination. This is important because it will help you to understand the impact when your enterprise changes direction (and it almost certainly will) and to track architecture change against business change.

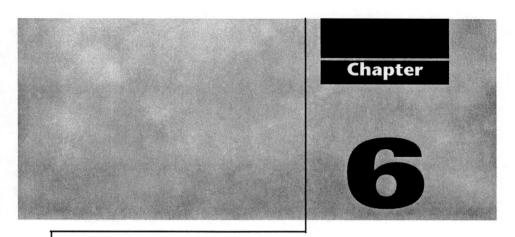

The Toolkit IT Framework: Principles

Once you have captured and analyzed where the business wants to go, how do you translate business opportunities into IT plans? That is the question we will begin to answer in this chapter.

The IT (Architecture) Framework

While the Toolkit begins with the practices required for collecting the correct input for architecture and ends with the practices required for implementing the architecture, we will focus in the next several chapters on the architecture itself. By "architecture" we mean the complete set of plans which guide the selection, construction, modification, and use of the enterprise information infrastructure to enable the desired business future state. For the purposes of our discussion, analysis and design are not within the scope of architecture, but we will illustrate the relationship between the two.

The Toolkit IT Framework (see Figure 6–1) is intended to provide a manageable table of contents for enterprise

45

architecture while intentionally limiting the scope of architecture. It defines the work the architect needs to do. It provides a roadmap for constructing *related IT infrastructure outputs* based on the business target state opportunities. The set of proscribed outputs constitutes an architecture—the complete (enough) set of IT plans. We believe that our framework is an adaptation of a CSC/Index Institute framework, but were never able to find any information about it.

The architecture outputs we discuss here are structurally *related* because the content of each *component* is associated with each other component and directly traceable to the business target state. We will see how the next steps of integration occur—the integration of business framework outputs into the IT framework and the integration of IT framework outputs with each other.

By "infrastructure" we mean all the products and services IT constructs, purchases, or uses to support the business. These include, but are not limited to, the databases, applications, hardware, and operational software and tools that IT builds, buys, and integrates or manages/outsources to run the business. We define "outputs" to mean individual, decoupled, reusable pieces (*components)* of infrastructure.

It is the related IT infrastructure components for which the architect will construct a roadmap or plan. The framework is intentionally simple. By purposefully limiting the scope of architecture, we are greatly increasing the likelihood that the architecture can be constructed and— just as important—actualized within a reasonable period of time.

In the model shown in Figure 6–1, which illustrates the framework, the rows describe IT plan components (data, functions, platform, and people) and the columns describe the required architecture outputs for the plan components. To create a complete, "good enough" IT enterprise architecture, we would develop each output for each component—fill in each cell.

For the purposes of this book:

- "Data" means key facts about the business;
- "Function" means a key operation necessary to run the business;
- "Platform" means the technology that enables the creation and use of the data and the functions; and,
- "People" refers to the consumers and/or providers of the data, the users of the functions, and the operators of the technology.

	Principles	Models	Inventory	Standards
Data				
Function				
Platform				
People/ Process				

Figure 6–1   The EA Toolkit IT Framework.

Defining Principles

In our IT Framework, "principles" represent the abstraction of the business target state to form guidelines for IT decision making. We use principles to translate the business target state into more generalized statements of direction for IT. For example, if business direction describes a need for more flexibility or faster time to market, we can translate that into a principle about the strong preference for reuseable pieces of IT infrastructure.

In many cases, we have seen organizations spend too much time in too many committee meetings arguing about the wording of principles. Often the outcome of all this disagreement leads to extremely wordy, long-winded documents that are unlikely to be followed—not to mention read. We have learned that it is more effective to have the team of architects brainstorm the basic ideas, perhaps send out a draft for comments—primarily to catch any missing fundamentals—and then quickly edit and publish. Principles, like other architecture outputs, can be updated as business change warrants.

Here are some guidelines for forming IT principles.

- Translate the business target statement to a statement of intent for IT (e.g., you could translate "CDCo wants to understand and better use customer buying information to leverage existing customer sales" to "Our customer information is our most valuable asset").

- Keep it short and sweet. If you want principles to be remembered and used, they should be no more than a sentence each (e.g., application functions will be reuseable).

- Use principles to communicate the basic tenets the company holds to be universally true. In most organizations we have worked with, there is some widely distributed document—like a goals or values statement—that contains these beliefs. This document may contain statements that can be directly translated to IT principles. A statement such as "Highly trained people are the key to our success" can be translated to an IT principle around the value of training and education.

- Use principles to impose business constraints on the models and standards you will develop (e.g., buy before you build).

- A set of principles should be contained to one page. A one-page set of principles is easier to distribute, read, and use. You will have plenty of opportunities to add architecture details when you create models, inventories, and standards.

The following are some examples of how IT principles are formed for each architecture component.

- *Data Principle* Data is owned by the corporation and not by any individual person or group.

- *Function Principle* Functions will be built or bought as reusable components.

- *Platform Principle* Vendor service is as important as product capability.

- *People Principle* The IT staff will be evaluated and compensated using common processes.

Remember the CDCo Statement of Goals for Y2000 from Chapter 2? They are provided below again for your reference:

CDCo Statement of Goals for Y2000

1. Learn more about our customers to better market to, retain, and satisfy them.
2. Increase the growth rate and revenue from music sales, and maintain the growth rate in publications.
3. Leverage the combined music/publications product lines.
4. Eliminate unnecessary expenses.
5. Become more open to change.
6. Invest in employee retention.
7. Leverage technology.

Here is an example of how we could translate the CDCo Statement of Goals into IT principles.

- *Data Principle*   Customer information is critical to the business. (1)
- *Function Principle*   Functions will be built or bought as reusable components. (4, 5)
- *Platform Principle*   Vendor viability is as important as product viability. (4, 7)
- *People Principle*   Employee training is a non-negotiable investment. (6)

CDCo IT Principles

The following is an example of a set of IT principles for CDCo.

- Information about our core business data—customers, products, orders and results—must be complete, accurate, timely and secure. (Goals 1, 2, and 3)
- Employee training is a non-negotiable investment. (6)
- Functions will be reusable so that we can easily and quickly respond to business change. (Goals 4 and 5)
- Technology will be selected based on architecture fit, capability, and vendor support. (Goals 5 and 7)

- Core information will be easily available to all departments. (Goal 1)
- Like other investments, IT components require business case analyses. (Goal 4)
- When solving new problems, we will leverage existing infrastructure. (Goals 4 and 5)
- We will buy before we build. (Goals 4 and 7)

In some cases we recommend that a single, integrated set of architecture outputs be created for all the components. This is true for principles and models. When it comes to inventory and standards, we believe it makes more sense to create a separate output for each component (e.g., a data inventory, technology standards). The single set of principles and models provides a sound basis for individual development of inventories and standards.

In Appendix B, we have included an additional example of a complete set of principles.

Suggested Exercise

Based on the outputs you created using the business framework, create a working draft of IT principles. Be sure to address data functions, platform/technology, and people.

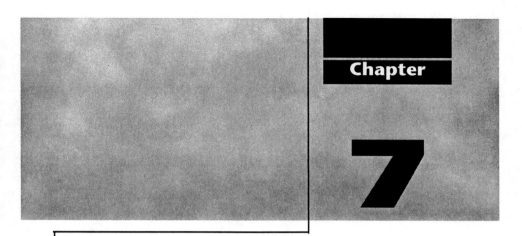

The Toolkit IT Framework: Architecture Models

What we have captured so far is fairly conceptual. Our next step is to take the needs and desires of the business, captured using the business framework and imbedded in principles, and begin to develop the details of the IT architecture. Eventually, the most detailed plans will become the blueprints for development. We will start with high-level architecture models and continue to develop more detailed architecture models to make that transition.

In our Toolkit, what we mean by an *architecture model* is the graphical representation of the *business view* of data, functions, technology, people, and the relationships and/or interactions between them. We address architecture modeling from two perspectives. The first has to do with context—your organization-specific environment and the expectations around creating architecture models—or ground rules. The second perspective is really a *how-to* of constructing architecture models.

51

Setting the Context for Architecture Models

Before you begin modeling, you must determine the organization's expectations and your objectives for developing architecture models. Use the questions below to determine how the models will be used in your organization:

- Who is the audience? What level-of-detail model do they need to see?
  - Business leaders?
  - Other planners, architects?
  - IT community?
- What will the content include?
  - Data, functions, technology, people?
  - Communications layers?
  - Technology?
  - Sequence? Flow?
- What planning horizons will be used?
  - Current State? One year? Three years? Five years?
- What part of IT does the architecture need to describe?
  - Execution environment (what the systems look like to the business)?
  - Development environment (infrastructure for programmers)?
  - Operations environment (infrastructure for data/network center)?
- How formal does the architecture documentation need to be?
  - Formal blueprinting?
  - No standards?

Ground Rules For Modeling

When you have answered these questions in the appropriate context for your organization, establish some *ground rules* before you actually build any architecture models. The rules we are about to describe are really standards for architecture modeling. The Toolkit *rules* we developed and still use are based on experience, so they are very practical.

Rule #1   Agree on a set of standard components.

Determine what types of IT infrastructure components you want to include in your architecture (e.g., data stores, servers). This may seem to be very basic advice, but we have never seen two architects include exactly the same components of architecture in a model in organizations that cannot agree on what components are to be modeled. Keep your organization in mind when selecting components. Your organization's structure or purpose may encourage you to use more or fewer components than our Toolkit does. For example, in a network-centric organization, you may want to add several specific network components (i.e., separately identifying switches from transport). In one organization we worked with, the Web was so important that it was treated as a separate component. As part of designating standard components, be sure to define each one.

Here are the standard Toolkit architecture components from which we construct all our architecture models. The following list of italicized components represent *politically-correct* components that we sometimes include in architecture models.

- *Architecture service*   Communication requirement between two or more architecture components (e.g., translation, messaging, transport)
- *Broker or hub*   Architecture service that translates, maps, and/or transports standard messages for common use
- *Business function*   Key operation necessary to run the business—minimally, a verb and a noun (e.g., Bill Customers); within the business function we also include Process, where it is applicable
- *Process*   Repeatable methods or tasks that support the people performing the function
- *Data store/database*   Key facts about the business stored for operational use
- *Data flow*   Key facts about the business exchanged between functions, interfaces, databases, data warehouses, interfaces, people, or architecture services
- *Data mart*   Function-specific subset of data warehouse, organized and stored to facilitate function-specific analysis, decision making, and reporting

- *Data warehouse*   Key facts about the business stored for analysis, decision making, and reporting
- *External interface*   Significant groups, places, things, systems, or event triggers outside of the organization that source, receive, or use data flows
- *People*   Consumers/providers of the data and the functions; customers, some suppliers, and groups of employee users are so critical to the business that we often depict them separately from other interfaces
- *Portal*   Gateway or access to other architecture components; a PC term for architecture service. We tend to use the concept of portal (versus intranet) when creating access to only certain components for a very specific group of users—like call center associates—whose access you may want to limit and whose interface needs to remain constant, even when back end change occurs or is being tested
- *Reference Data*   Small set (few columns) of relatively static data shared across many business functions, often consisting of codes (e.g., account codes), abbreviations (state codes), *type* or *model* data (more on this later)

In our models, we include key technology by assigning *platform* to individual components:

- *Platform*   Key technology used to enable an architecture service, business function, data store, data warehouse, or interface where appropriate—includes hardware, software, network, DBMS, etc.

When selecting standard components, keep your organization's purpose in mind. For example, in a network-centric organization (e.g., telecom, IT), you might want break down *architecture service* and specifically include some network services, like transport or switching.

Rule #2   Use a standard representation scheme.

You will make your job much easier if you establish a standard representation of each architecture component you have chosen to include in your standard set. By using a standard set of symbols or icons to represent architecture components and any additional desired notations, your architecture modeling symbols will always have the same meaning. Without standards for representing components, it is unlikely that any two architects will use the same representation to convey the same intent. Having a single scheme is an advantage because it allows discussion of the quality of the architecture versus the meaning or intention of a particular symbol. And, hopefully, architecture quality is what will facilitate meeting the business needs.

For the Toolkit, we began with Gane & Sarson *Data Flow Diagrams* function and interface symbols, and added some additional icons to represent components and some basic architecture notations (see Figure 7–1). This is an intentionally simple set of graphical notations, and you may choose to add or remove symbols as needed. While a more complex system of notations would allow for more architectural precision, our experience has shown that the time required to model with extreme precision outweighs the benefits achieved (not to mention the time allotted).

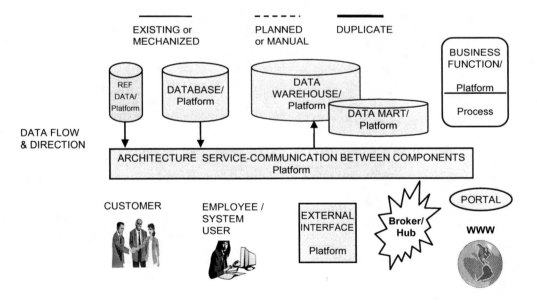

Figure 7–1   Toolkit standard architecture modeling notations.

Rule #3 Set a scope.

Determine what key architecture components are combined with, included in, or excluded from an individual architecture model. We have created technology-only or data-only architecture models on some occasions (see Figure 7–2). Based on experience, including all the key components (data, function, technology, and people) in every architecture model works best. While architecture models that include all components are somewhat more complex, they require the architect to consider integration at every step of construction. Another advantage of addressing all components in individual models is that it allows architecture team members to work on inventories and standards based on a common set of models.

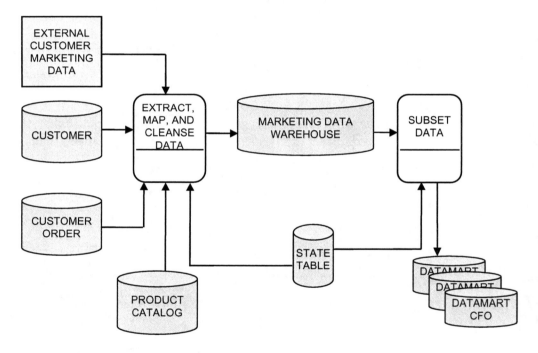

Figure 7–2 A data-only architecture model.

Rule #4   Determine the level of detail.

Determine the level of an individual model that is appropriate for your purpose and audience. We recommend creating multiple levels of architecture models. One advantage of *leveling* is that it provides a way to simplify each model while maintaining the integration achieved by including all components. The levels of detail included in the Toolkit follow.

- *Level 0*   This is a conceptual, one-page model of key infrastructure components and their relationships. A conceptual model is used to communicate overall *state*. It is most often used with a business audience or as an introduction to the architecture to communicate fundamental concepts.

- *Level 1*   This is a more detailed, specific view of part of a Level 0 model and is used to communicate direction.

- *Level n*   This is the most detailed level of an architecture model. Level *n* models form the *bridge* from architecture to development by communicating decisions. Level *n* models provide the detail needed by designers and developers to translate architecture to systems requirements and designs.

- *Presentation Level*   In the Toolkit, we recommend that the executive presentation of the architecture is a requirement to confirm architecture direction. To make the architecture meaningful to the executives, it is often necessary to construct a separate Presentation-Level model. The Presentation-Level model is constructed at an even higher level and is even further abstracted than a Level 0 model. It usually includes only significant components—those which require funded projects to implement.

It is generally necessary to develop models at all the levels described here to put together a complete package for all the audiences with which you need to communicate:

- *The business*   Level 0 to communicate, discuss, and receive feedback on concepts

- *Systems analysts*   Level 1 to communicate direction for research and analysis

- *IT designers and developers* — Level *n* to communicate decisions that require compliance
- *Decision makers* — Presentation Level to communicate what needs support and funding

Rule #5   Define the state to be modeled.

An architecture model is much like a snapshot. The state describes the point in time reflected in the model. For example:

- Current state (as is)
- Target state (will be)
- End-of-year state (business plan)
- 2001 Migration Plan (interim or migration view)

Figure 7–3 illustrates a target state architecture model.

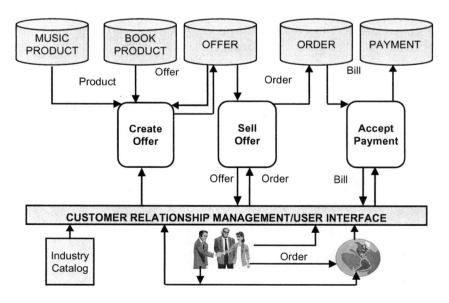

Figure 7–3   Part of CDCo Level 0 target state architecture model using Toolkit standard notations.

Chapter **7** | Architecture Models

Rule #6 Define the environment.

Define the environment portrayed in an individual model. The environment describes the layer of IT that is being modeled. I have often seen (and early on created) models that were describing *apples and oranges*—similar to what a residential architect might create if he included part of a house and part of the sewer system in the same blueprint. Environments that you ought to separate in architecture models are indicated in Figure 7–4 and include the following:

- *Execution environment* This is the set of architecture components used to run the enterprise (i.e., the components—data stores, functions, architecture services—required to support key business applications like ordering and billing, human resources, and accounting).

- *Development environment* This is the set of architecture components required to support the development staff (e.g., programming language compilers and testing tools).

- *Operations environment* This is the set of architecture components required to monitor and manage the health of the IT infrastructure (e.g., a Network Operating System (NOS) or a server capacity monitoring tool).

Your models will be more clear and useful to individual audiences if each environment and its unique functions, data stores, interfaces, and other architecture components are modeled separately.

Building Architecture Models

Now that we have established a set of modeling ground rules, we will look at how to translate the business framework outputs to architecture models. We will begin with the Toolkit guidelines for constructing Level 0 models. For the current state, constructing at least a Level 0 architecture model provides a lot of value. It is a very useful tool for portraying what problems exist, and, depending on the size of your infrastructure, can also be used as a form of current state inventory (more about this later).

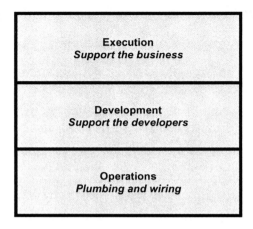

Figure 7–4   The IT architecture environment.

Level 0 Current State Model

While existing models of legacy infrastructure can be useful as input for constructing a current state architecture model, they are often inadequate as substitutes. Most current state legacy models we have seen focus on boxes (servers, network) rather than on business applications, data, interfaces, and services. To construct a Level 0 Current State model, we translate the business current state description's key facts to high-level architecture components. You might want to list each of the outputs for the following steps before you actually begin to construct a model.

1. Identify the major *interfaces* that provide or use data—key customers, suppliers, industry regulators, external systems (e.g., customer).
2. Define the *data flow*—file, message, manual input, transaction, etc.—each interface receives or sources (e.g. payment).
3. Define what operation a *function* performs on each data flow—a verb-noun combination—(e.g. Validate Payment).
4. Designate *stored data* (e.g., Accounts Receivable).

Chapter **7** I Architecture Models

5. Determine where *communication or services*—translation, mapping, transport, routing, etc.—exist between components (e.g. User Interface between Customer Order and Calculate Bill).

6. Create *data flows* between functions and stored data or services where appropriate (e.g., Customer Payment).

Figure 7–5 illustrates the how these steps would be translated to a Level 0 current state architecture model for CDCo.

Although I have worked with organizations that opt not to build current state architecture models, I have found them to be extremely useful. While everyone in your organization may understand that the current IT environment is complex, tightly coupled, and contains many redundancies, an accurate model can be a powerful marketing tool. A current state model makes suspected or intuited problems obvious. Another benefit of current state modeling is that it provides a benchmark against which you can evaluate the proposed target state. For example: Is the target state truly more simple or less coupled than the current state?

Considerations for Assessing Current State Architecture

Once you have collected or captured the current state architecture in models, you may want to use some of these questions to analyze its strengths and weaknesses, and plan for the target state.

1. How can the legacy infrastructure investment be leveraged?

   The current useful life of a mission-critical application today is probably *less than* five years (although some current studies we have seen are looking at seven years) because of the speed of business and technology changes. But you may have some older infrastructure you want to consider including in your target because it performs its function well and can be adapted to work with your target at minimal expense.

2. Are the products standard and high-quality?

   To determine whether or not you should replace current products, consider how products are recommended in independent reviews (e.g., the Gartner Group's *Enterprise DBMS Vendor Magic Quadrant* includes DBMS and Platform).

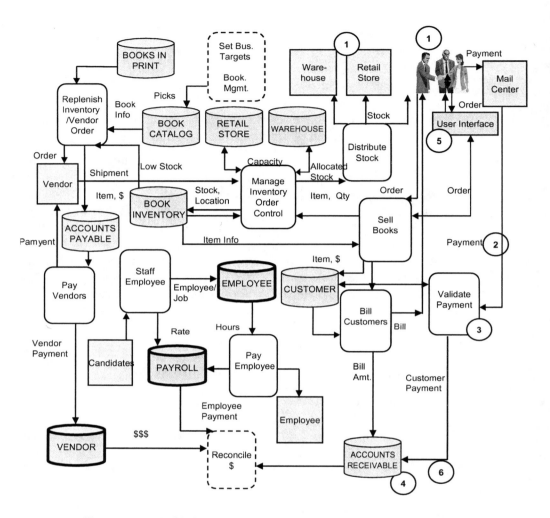

Figure 7–5   A CDCo level 0 current state architecture model.

Choose platforms that receive the highest ratings versus platforms that may be described as "still need to convince and prove... [they are] suitable for large, mission-critical applications."[1] Where possible, choose or retain products that are aligned with standards (e.g., XML, JAVA).

1. E. Brown, "Internet Middleware Analysis," *Forrester TechStragegy Report*, Aug. 3, 1999.

3. How tightly coupled is the architecture?

   If key pieces of infrastructure are highly coupled, you may want to consider replacing them with architecture components/layers that are loosely coupled so future changes—and replacements when necessary—are feasible and affordable.

4. Does the current state allow for integration?

   I would look beyond stored procedures to some additional forms of Enterprise Application Integration (EAI). The overall logical architecture—functions, data, services (e.g., communications)—should be layered to allow for loose coupling. EAI should be used for messaging/communication and translation between layers (e.g., between GUI and application services). EAI should be considered for business process automation (very high-level process flow management). For example, process automation could be used to mechanize process scheduling and reporting. EAI does not have to be physically implemented in the first/next release of architecture, but the logical architecture ought to incorporate EAI-based concepts. EAI is supported by many products you may already own (not compared here).

5. What is the data center impact of architecture change?

   If you have spare capacity, lots of experience, and few operational problems in data center support for an existing industrial-strength platform, do not underestimate the impact of changing platforms. When the set of operational capabilities and systems management capabilities (backup, recovery, storage management, scheduling and workload management, and disaster recovery) are completely integrated, tried, and true, you may already have in place all that is essential for mission-critical applications.

6. Does it meet today's basic requirements?

   For example, do you already have a conventional, proven environment (scores or hundreds of successfully implemented enterprise applications) with plenty of scalability, security, and reliability?

7. Does your current architecture support a short *time-to-market* for new business applications?

   In addition to platform choices, there are some key architectural approaches that also impact time-to-market, scalability, and responsiveness to change. Some current *architecture capabilities* ought to be considered as part of your study—not necessarily physically, but in how the logical components are intended to work together. The recommendation here is to ensure the architecture model accounts for these components. Physical implementation can be planned for later phases. For example, an immediate CRM capability could be limited to the development of a strategy for creating a tighter bond with the customer, or to a project to improve the quality of customer data.

8. How flexible is the current architecture?

   Given the speed of business change, the importance of flexibility cannot be overlooked. The logical architecture, including the middleware *glue*, can *make or break* the ability of the business to respond to change.[2] Middleware is the foundation for EAI, although you could begin to integrate "islands of information"[3] using messaging. Again, the early implementation of EAI can be limited to a review of the existing capabilities you already *own*. Existing transactions can be used as initial messages. The business process automation capability of EAI (high-level process flow management) can be evaluated to replace manual scheduling and the triggering of functions. You can begin to move to *logical* EAI by decoupling components, and you can begin to provide basic communication between architecture layers, for example, by reusing existing interfaces.

9. How important is e-Business?

   If the answer is *very important*, then logical architecture again plays a key role. In addition to enterprise-strength platform components, it becomes increasingly important to focus on the management of key data stores.[4] You may choose to do this through empowering a strong data management organization, through the data mapping and translation capabilities of an EAI solution and/or through minimal common data standards. An early project here might be the assessment of the accessibility and accuracy of customer data on the Web versus in legacy databases, or an evaluation of your current ability to respond to customers through their channels of choice (e.g., Web versus call

---

[2.] M. Stonebraker, "Integrating Islands of Information: A New Look at EAI," *EAI Journal*, Feb. 24, 2000

[3.] Ibid.

[4.] M. S. McGarr, "Y2K Paves the Way for Enterprise E-Commerce," *ECommerce World*, Feb. 1, 2000

center). A more complex project would put these two together to assess customer information accessibility via the Internet versus legacy applications and databases.

Level 0 Target State Model

After you have documented the current state and considered some of the preceding questions, it is appropriate to undertake the development of the target state architecture. To begin to construct a Level 0 *Target State* architecture model, translate business opportunities to infrastructure components as follows.

1. Extract the opportunities you identified while doing the business target state analysis; use the following for example.

   - *Current*   Service offerings can expand through the acquisition of Bookseller.

   - *Target*   Customers can order any combination of products and pay online.

   - *Opportunity*   Develop offers of combos of book/music products; make offers available online.

2. Then, translate the opportunity to infrastructure components and list them. In this example, several infrastructure components are implied:

   - CDCo and Bookseller Product data stores, a Combo Offer data store

   - A function that creates/updates Offers

   - A function that accepts online payment (e.g., credit card, account debit)

   - Website access to Offers

   - Modification/addition of user interface

3. Next, we want to transfer the identified components to a Level 0 target state architecture model. The following are some guidelines we use.

   - Look for desired future state interfaces (e.g., new external sources of book and recording titles). Do not include interfaces you will eliminate (we can take care of these in *migration models*).

- Define desired future state data flows—future state inputs and outputs (e.g., data flow of titles from new interface).
- Place key existing functions and add new functions relative to the future roles of interfaces, customers, and suppliers (e.g., a new Create Offer function).
- Place key data stores or data warehouses relative to future key functions (e.g., a New Offer data store is available to the ordering function).
- Add architecture services where they should exist (e.g., a user interface, data access services).
- Where known, add key enabling technologies as conceptual services (e.g., messaging, CRM).
- Where known, reflect substantive people changes (e.g., a different title or group of employees interacting via the Web).

Figure 7–6 illustrates the Level 0 Target State Execution Environment Architecture Model for CDCo. You have probably noticed the long-winded titles our models have. This is because we want to label exactly what the model represents.

Architecture Strategies

Very often, if you have discussed or considered adding architecture services, creating new functions, regrouping data, or investigating new technologies, what you are really doing is beginning to define strategies for the target architecture. So, while models are necessary and extremely useful, you need to consider augmenting them with strategy documents. Here we are referring to a short story versus a novel. We recommend creating a small set of very succinct statements or brief position papers that each address a specific strategy (e.g., data management, messaging). The document should focus on the *what* and *why* rather than the *how* (this can be addressed when you develop standards). Strategies are more precise than principles and models and help clarify the intentions implicit in target architecture models.

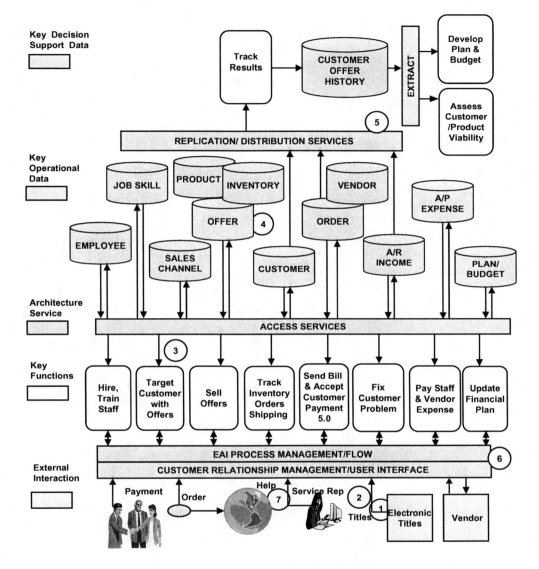

Figure 7–6   A CDCo level 0 target state architecture model.

It is appropriate, therefore, to address the purpose or intent of the new or changed approach, how it will improve IT support of the business target state (e.g., it will replace or eliminate a current problematic solution), the high-level costs and benefits, and the proposed fit/form of the architecture in a document of a few pages. For example, if you are defining a messaging strategy, you may want to include whether your model is hub or broker, if messages will be *pushed* or *pulled*, how messaging will replace hundreds or thousands of pair-wise interfaces, the potential speed and accuracy benefits for the business, and a high-level estimate of initial costs and the time needed to implement messaging.

Appendix C includes sample concepts for architecture strategies. While they are somewhat specific, they provide examples of the kinds of architecture intentions you might want to consider documenting.

Level 1 Model

Because it is almost impossible to create more than a very conceptual high-level model in one picture, our next task is to begin to describe the architecture in more detail. One way to add detail is to decompose or *level* the model one or more iterations. Several approaches we have used for leveling or decomposing a Level 0 model include:

- Subsetting by target function (e.g., all the subfunctions and related data and services associated with Billing)
- Subsetting by architecture service (e.g., all subservices, data, and functions that interact with the Data Management service)
- Subsetting by target data area (e.g., all the data stores, services, and functions related to Customer data)

To decompose your Level 0 model to a Level 1 model subsetting by function, try the following steps.

1. List the function steps or tasks (subfunctions).
2. Document where formal processes exist.
3. Examine the sequence/dependencies.
4. Determine what data, interfaces, services, and flows are involved.

Figure 7–7a shows the part of the Level 0 model to be leveled; Figure 7–7b shows the Level 1 model that results from applying the steps above.

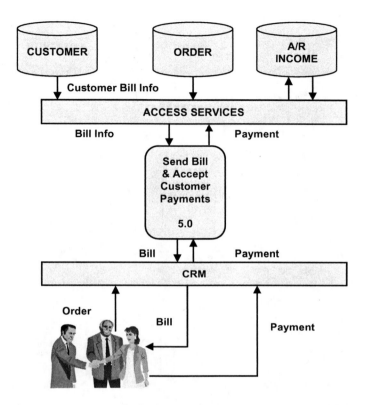

Figure 7–7a A slice of CDCo Level 0 target state architecture model with "Send Bill" function.

If you are going to decompose a Level 1 model by subsetting an architecture service, try these steps.

1. Define all the functions the service must perform (subservices).

2. Define the new data required to perform the service functions.

3. Refine the connections between the services/service functions and the other architecture components (data, business functions, etc.).

4. Consider adding technology/technology function at this level.

Figure 7–8a shows an architecture service to be decomposed from a Level 0 model. Figure 7–8b shows the Level 1 model that results from applying the steps above.

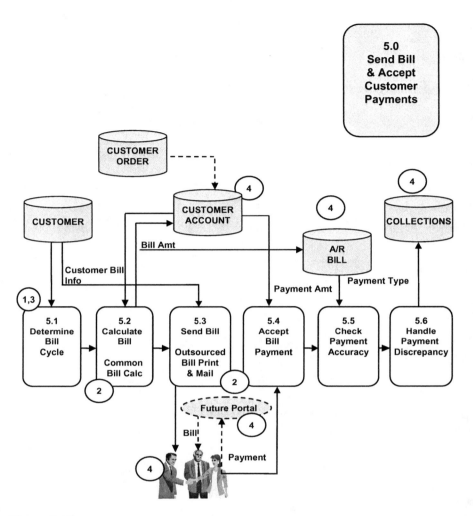

Figure 7–7b A CDCo Level 1 target state architecture model for send bill function.

While we have used all of these approaches when developing architecture models, we prefer to subset Level 0 models by target data area. We have found that when core enterprise data is examined and decomposed, it tends to lead to the identification of a very complete set of the functions and services required to process, transform, and manage it.

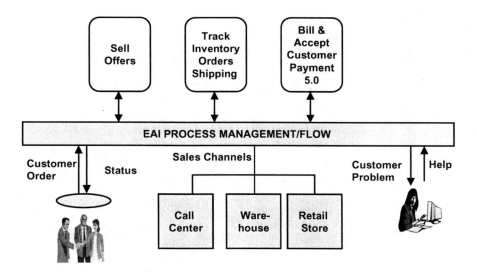

Figure 7–8a A slice of CDCo level 0 target state architecture model with EAI service.

Here are the steps we follow:

1. Select a major data area from the Level 0 model (e.g., Customer, Employee).

2. Break that area into logical subsets. Use the terms found in the business target state analysis for direction (e.g., Customer Demographics, Customer Account, and Customer Invoice). There should be exclusivity across the subsets, but these are still *logical* subsets—not yet at an atomic level (or even at the data entity level). Use business terms in your model.

3. Determine which target subfunctions are required to update/access each subset.

4. Define how the data will be sourced and accessed (e.g., Customer accesses Bill via the Web). This is a good place to begin identifying common services to manage data.

5. Link the functions/services to the interfaces that will provide/use the data (e.g., Supplier provides Supplier Invoice).

6. Consider what type of data is needed. This is a good place to consider discriminating between operational and decision support, reference data, etc. You may also want to begin to add technology at this level (e.g., RDBMS).

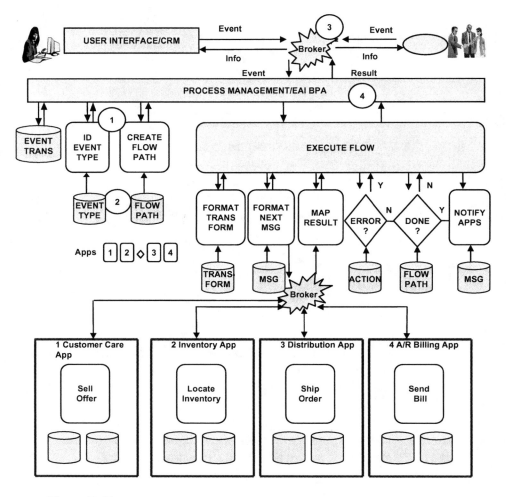

Figure 7–8b A CDCo Level 1 architecture model for EAI service.

Figure 7–9a shows an example of a part of a Level 0 model to be decomposed.

Figure 7–9b shows the Level 1 model that results from the decomposition.

We have had workshop students ask why we did not recommend decomposing models using all the approaches just discussed at once. In my experience, it is both more "do-able" and more straight-forward to choose a single approach. An added advantage is that the resulting models can be more easily tested to find and evaluate gaps and overlaps—much like putting sections of a jig-saw puzzle back together.

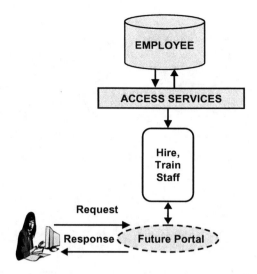

Figure 7–9a A slice of CDCo Level 0 target state architecture model with an employee.

Level *n* Models

How can you tell when you are *finished* decomposing architecture models? When have you reached Level *n*? We have said that our scope is IT architecture—strategy and planning—rather than analysis or design/development. Here are some clues that you have completed architecture modeling and are beginning to encroach on analysis/design.

- Functions are beginning to look like module/object designs.
- Data store names are beginning to sound like logical data entities or tables.
- Architecture services are so discretely identified that each one could be replaced by a specific product.

Figure 7–10 shows a decomposed Level 1 model that appears to have gone too far.

By the time you have reached Level *n* modeling, you will want (or may have already begun) to give some thought to architecture patterns—how different pieces of the target architecture ought to be grouped into layers and applications, and what characteristics of those applications ought to drive development. Appendix D includes examples of architecture patterns.

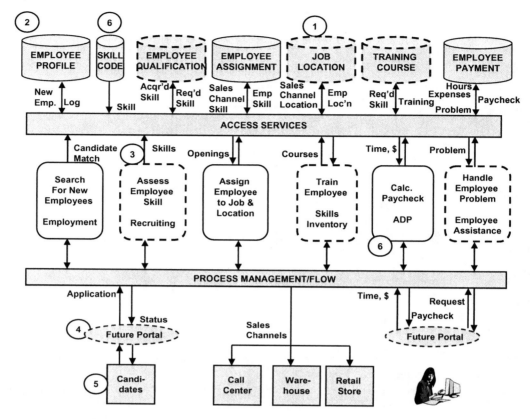

Figure 7–9b   A CDCo Level 1 target state architecture model for employee data.

Suggested Exercise

If you have not already created a rough draft of a Level 0 target state architecture model, you may want to stop and do so for your execution (run-the-business) environment.

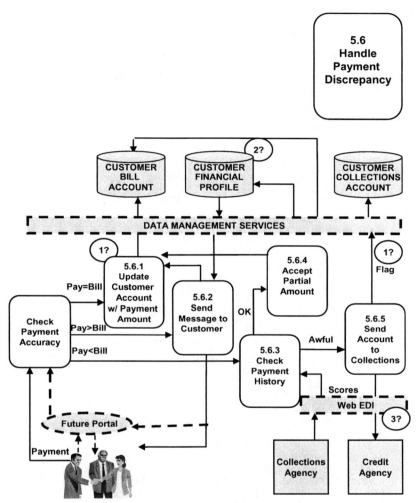

Figure 7–10   A CDCo Level 2 target state architecture model for the "Handle Payment Discrepancy" function.

Architecture-Based Logical Models

We said earlier that analysis and design were separate processes from architecture. We would like to use *data* as an example of where architecture ends and systems analysis and design begin, and also to illustrate how architecture outputs need to be related to—in fact, ought to drive—analysis and design outputs. There needs to be the same, strong relationship between the architect and application development and between the architect and the technologists.

Relative to logical data modeling, we often find the following.

- The terms *data architecture* and *data model* are used interchangeably.
- The data architecture function is isolated from the "real" architecture (the technology architecture or, occasionally, the application architecture).
- The data model is constructed before, or without reference to, the enterprise architecture.
- The data management organization is viewed as a set of eccentric folks with ersatz skill sets who are not nearly as vital to IT as the developers and database administrators.
- And, somehow, IT projects continue to fail.

On the off chance that you are one of the heads-down, microscopically focused data modelers among whom I used to dwell—or more likely, that you are an information manager who is having trouble persuading his fellows to *do it right*, allow us to offer a glimmer of hope. We believe there is a strong and necessary relationship between the architect and the data manager, and that by working together they can have a profound impact on IT implementations and ultimately on business success (assuming this is in some way relevant to our income).

Although I began my career as a programmer just before the end of the Punic Wars, and modeled data towards the beginning of the American Civil War, I have come—over time and through unsought opportunity—to see the value and the business benefits of information planning at the enterprise level, especially that which is undertaken prior to *pinning down the details*. Using IT resources to develop an information plan is not always an easy sell—data has never been as "sexy" as technology. In the past couple of years, however, we have seen an intensified interest in both information management and architecture—even beyond the CIO level. That interest, we believe, is the place where we must begin to overcome past mistakes.

That mouthful having been said, what we are proposing next is to create the often missing link between enterprise architecture and data modeling. Figure 7–11 shows how the two sides line up.

Enterprise Architecture Model	Data Model
Business View of IT	IT View of Business
Strategic View	Logical View
Planning Phase	Analysis Phase
Relationship of Data to Business Functions, External Interfaces, Services, Technologies/Strategies	Relationship of data to other data
Key Data Interactions, Capture and Storage	Data Structure
Art?	Science?

Figure 7–11   The architecture model versus the data model.

We believe that the data architecture must precede the data (application and technology) modeling, and that the roles of architecture and logical modeling are very different, as compared in Figure 7–9a. The role of architecture is to describe what the key data is, its source and purpose for the business, how it needs to be used (e.g., operational versus analytic), and how it needs to relate to other architecture components.

When the gaps between the architecture model and the logical models are not bridged, the result may be technically excellent but useless outputs. When we developed the target architecture that was required to support the business going forward in one organization, it was an almost impossible task to reverse engineer the enterprise data model. In another organization, the purchase of an external data model was proposed prior to defining what the target architecture should be. Similarly, we have seen clients purchase packaged applications or tools without having a target architecture in place against which to evaluate appropriateness. Is it any wonder that we do analysis against our operational databases and run operational processes using data from the warehouse, and that the business remains mistrustful of IT?

Based on our experiences—the good, the bad, and the ugly—we have devised and successfully used some very practical approaches designed to support both the architecture and data modeling efforts, and for providing a working translation from one to the other. The following list details those approaches.

- Make sure your enterprise architecture includes business functions and key information. If your architecture is simply a technology plan, throw it away and start over. The plan needs to include the function, data, and technology components of the business and how they are related.

- Use business language in the architecture. If the business calls them "Clients," do not refer to them as "Customers" in the architecture. There is plenty of time to precisely name objects in the data model.

- Get business and IT concurrence on the architecture before you proceed any further. Any lack of time spent here is sure to cost 10 times as much in data modeling.

- Use the architecture model as the basis for the conceptual data model (Toolkit definition: the one-page, entity-relationship model that describes the relationship of each set of data included in the architecture model to every other set).

- Include business policies—high-level written practices or guidelines that describe how the business wants to operate on the information. For example: "Different sales channels (store, phone, and Web) will require different job skills. Over time, an employee may gain proficiency in many job skills and be assigned to different sales channels."

- Set standards—names and definitions for the entities.

- Because this is a one-page model, there should only be a few (not many) entities that require standards, and these should be the basic information blocks of the organization (e.g., Customer, Product, and Employee). Spend your time on defining the few, core identifiers that will be the basis for more detailed modeling. More about standards in Chapter 9.

- Get business and IT concurrence on the conceptual data model. Wherever possible, use the same participants who reviewed the architecture model. If they do not understand it, then it is not a conceptual data model or it is not an accurate translation. Revise as necessary.

- Consider *just-in-time* logical modeling. Develop detailed models as new projects warrant.
- Publish or perish. Make sure the models are available to architects, database designers, and developers.

This is a fairly simple—but not necessarily easy—process to execute. You are likely to meet resistance, which is why the concurrence steps are so important, and often so time-consuming. In later chapters we will discuss some practical strategies for gaining concurrence, but if you undertake these steps you will have put in place all the necessary linkages to translate the business requirements to architecture, to translate the architecture to data models, and to provide the data models for translation code and databases. These same steps need to be applied to application development, technology implementation, and human resources' (HR) plans for IT. By following this process, you will actually enable the delivery of IT components that meet the business goals—and that, ultimately is why we work in IT.

Translating Architecture to Conceptual Data Model

Let us take the linkage of architecture to design one step further. We will use data as the example, although the translation process described here needs to also be applied to applications, technology, and IT HR. For our example we will look at how to translate an architecture model to a conceptual data model.

Our definition of a conceptual data model is the translation of lowest-level target state architecture model data areas to conceptual mega-entities. This creates the bridge that begins the transition from architecture to analysis. The architect should play a strong role in this transition.

Follow these steps to develop a conceptual data model.

1. List the target data areas—the large, uncoupled sets of objects described in the architecture models in business terms (e.g., customer, staff).

2. Translate logical data subsets created in the *lowest-level* target state architecture model to conceptual mega-entities (not

atomic)—the persons, places, things, relationships, and events about which the business cares enough to document.

3. Represent the mega-entities in a simplified Entity Relationship Diagram and edit—add or divide—the entities.

4. Define business policies—high-level written practices or guidelines that describe how the business wants to operate on the information. These are not yet at the *term, fact, and rule* level (not atomic).

The following are examples of CDCo policies.

- Different sales channels (store, phone, Web) will require different job skills.
- The skills inventory process is used to determine if an employee has the requisite job skill(s) to be assigned to a sales channel.
- Over time, an employee may gain proficiency in many job skills and be assigned to different sales channels.
- Sales channels will be expanded to new locations and types.
- Set Standards—names, definitions, and a logical structure for the entity identifiers (much more about standards later).

The following are examples of a CDCo standard.

- *Employee*   Any person permanently hired by CDCo to perform tasks or services for which s/he receives a regular weekly CDCo paycheck. An Employee is uniquely identified by a Badge Number.

Figure 7–12 represents the simplified, conceptual Entity Relationship Diagram (ERD) for CDCo.

For data, the next logical step (no pun intended) is the creation of the logical data model—a more detailed, fully normalized view of the data, including metadata, entity and attribute definitions, and rules to provide guidance for database design. I do not believe it is the job of the enterprise architect to create the logical data models. This is where the data analysts should take the reins. If the architect has created or participated in the creation of the conceptual enterprise data model, and established high-level core business data definitions (e.g., Customer, Product), then the data analysts will have a solid foundation on which to build. The architects should complete this cycle by reviewing the

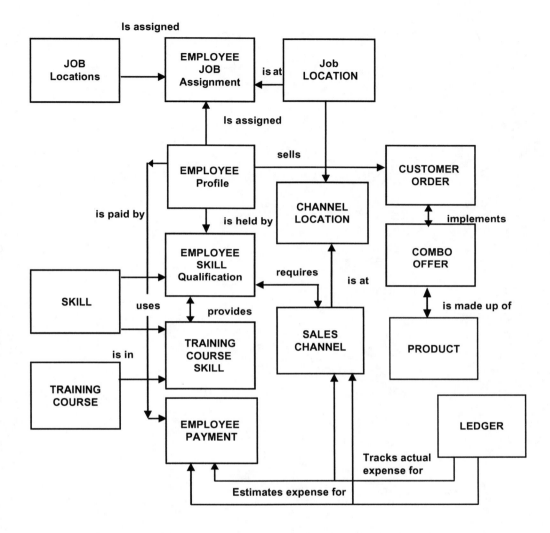

Figure 7–12   A part of CDCo conceptual data model.

logical data models to ensure they have not deviated significantly from the target architecture intent. The same approach needs to be used to translate architecture to system and technology design and to review the design outputs. We will talk more about architecture review of analysis and design when we discuss architecture governance in Chapter 13.

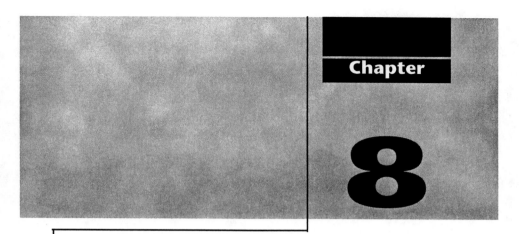

8

The Toolkit IT Framework: Inventory

It still surprises us when we come across organizations that do not create and maintain a formal IT inventory, but many do not. While it may seem tedious to construct, we have found IT inventories to be a valuable tool—and remarkably effective in making the case for architecture, including funding for architecture. That is partly true because we believe you should always include the costs of inventory items—the financials associated with inventory assets.

The Toolkit definition of IT inventory is the listing of all the key IT resources of the organization—data, applications, platform/technology, and people assets—and their key attributes. Because constructing an inventory can be time consuming, we strongly recommend that you set objectives for your inventory so you can attack what is most important in your organization. Many of the same basic rules and decisions that apply to architecture *models* apply to architecture *inventory,* as shown below.

- Set a scope.
- Determine level of detail.

- Define state.
- Define the environment.
- Agree on a format.

Set a Scope

Determine what components are combined, included in, and excluded from an individual architecture inventory (e.g., the contents of a single cell). Because the characteristics of each component (data, platform, etc.) are so different, we usually create a separate inventory for each cell component (unlike our approach to principles and models).

For example, we created the following for CDCO:

- A data inventory table for key data stores;
- An application (function) inventory—a detailed physical architecture model of all applications used by more than one retail outlet or channel;
- A platform inventory spreadsheet for all CDCo and Bookseller technology; and
- A skills inventory listing for each CDCo and Bookseller employee.

Determine the Level of Detail

The following are a few factors to consider when deciding at what level of detail you will develop inventories:

- *Inclusivity*   In a very large organization it may not be possible to locate every data store, every software module, type of PC software, skill, etc. For example, you can determine before you begin that you will only include key pieces—those that have a relationship with multiple data stores, applications, or organizations. Maintaining an inventory can be very time-

consuming and even basic information provides plenty of
support for good decision making.

- *Properties* There are many unique characteristics you could
  describe about each piece of the technology platform (e.g.,
  height and weight) or each application (e.g., lines of code).
  When undertaking an inventory where none exists, it is usually
  preferable to focus on the collection of a few key characteristics
  (e.g., platform item—name, model number, vendor, quantity,
  price, location/organization).

- *Model or Item* For platform inventory, determine if the
  inventory should list only the *model* (e.g., 3M Renaissance
  mouse) or the specific item/occurrence (the 3M Renaissance
  mouse sitting in my office). The larger the organization and the
  greater its assets, the more desirable it becomes to limit the
  inventory members to models and counts. This is especially true
  for lower-cost items.

- *Brief Commercial Break* We recommend that basic content
  should always include the cost/price. The inventory then
  becomes not only a tool for describing how expensive it is to
  maintain the current state, but provides the groundwork for
  measuring how effective the architecture is.

Define the State

There are reasons to document both current and target state inventories. If you are limited in what you can create by time or resources, here
are some suggestions.

- *Data Inventory* Focus on the current state. This can really
  support your modeling effort and provide information that is
  extremely useful in positioning the target state for funding. A
  current state data inventory can later be modified to create a
  target state inventory, since this is usually the result of
  consolidation and replacement.

- *Application Inventory* Focus on the current state for the same
  reasons as previously stated.

- *Platform Inventory*   Focus on current and target states. A current state, item-level inventory is necessary for managing and tracking major assets. A target state, model-level inventory is highly desirable for describing and publishing what the standard environment is intended to be. It is also a good place to describe which technology is being retired, which is being tested, and which is truly target.
- *People/Processes Inventory*   Focus on the current state. This is especially important when describing employee skills and job roles. This data can be used to forecast shortages, fill positions, and plan training.

Define the Environment

In most cases inventory should be done for all three environments—execution, development, and operations—since each requires different data stores, applications, platform technology, and skills/roles. Creating separate inventories for each environment, or to at least subsetting an inventory by environment, facilitates clarity (what is being described) and usefulness (e.g., for publication or presentation). Figure 8–1 shows an example of subsetting inventory by environment for CDCo.

Agree on a Format

The format for each component inventory need not be the same. It is more important that you determine the scope, level of detail, etc., of what will be included and how broadly you intend for the inventory to be used. If time permits, use a standardized inventory format—by component—and consider capturing inventory in a text or graphic format. The size of your infrastructure, available resources, and intended use can guide the selection of a format for your organization. Some examples of formats for data/application inventory follow.

- *Detailed Design Models*   This is a set of design models illustrating each application and every interfacing data store. In one case we developed and maintained an application inventory

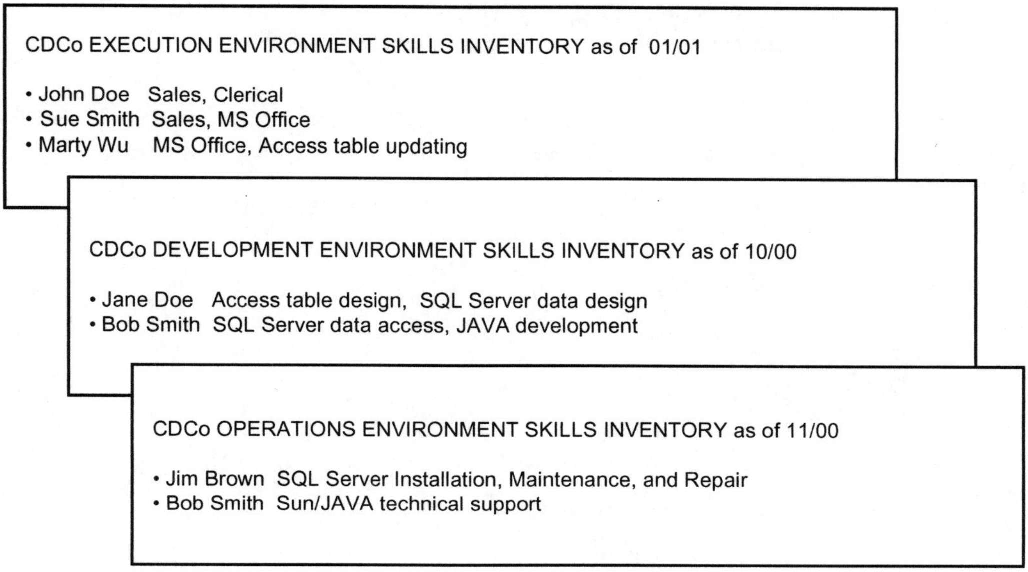

CDCo EXECUTION ENVIRONMENT SKILLS INVENTORY as of 01/01

• John Doe   Sales, Clerical
• Sue Smith Sales, MS Office
• Marty Wu   MS Office, Access table updating

CDCo DEVELOPMENT ENVIRONMENT SKILLS INVENTORY as of 10/00

• Jane Doe   Access table design, SQL Server data design
• Bob Smith SQL Server data access, JAVA development

CDCo OPERATIONS ENVIRONMENT SKILLS INVENTORY as of 11/00

• Jim Brown SQL Server Installation, Maintenance, and Repair
• Bob Smith Sun/JAVA technical support

Figure 8–1   Inventory scope.

of more than 500 major applications in a book of models (one page per application). For each application we included a physical current state model of the application and its data and interfaces, and a few key pieces of descriptive information. In this format the inventory tended to be used as a reference handbook for the entire development community.

- *Summary Architecture Model*   This is a single, physical current state model describing every *major* application and database (at least a Level 1 model). While this type of model is not an *easy read*, it can be effective for use as a summary/reference document for a small or medium-sized organization.

- *Table*   This is a list of data stores or applications and key descriptors. In a medium-sized organization, for example, we developed a three-page table for architects and designers that listed about 100 databases.

While a data inventory can contain a complete list of all the data resources of the business—automated databases, internal and external data flows, manual and automated files and spreadsheets, reference tables, graphical product specifications, and other critical documents—here is an example of the inventory decisions we made for the resource-constrained, current state execution environment data inventory for CDCo.

- *Inclusivity*   For CDCo, we included only *critical* data resources (e.g., we did not capture every retail-store-specific spreadsheet).
- *Properties*   We had limited time and resources, so we only included:
  - Name/type of data
  - Data store acronym/physical name
  - Technology
  - *Data Store of Record* designation where possible for every major data store (and external source data flow)
  - Volume/record size
  - Cost (one-time and ongoing)

When we have more resources available, we will add:

- The physical location of the data;
- The data steward/owner if assigned;
- Access keys; and
- Accessing applications.

To sum things up, the bottom line is that if your organization or business is very large or complex, we recommend selecting simpler formats—including basic content and aiming for *complete enough*.

Figure 8–2 illustrates the CDCo Data Inventory.

Suggested Exercise

List the characteristics you would like to include in an applications inventory for your business. If one already exists, list the modifications you would like to make.

DATA AREA	FILE NAME/ ANNUAL EXPENSE	ACRONYM	VOLUME/SIZE	TECHNOLOGY
Product	Books In Print $0.7 Mil.	BIP	5,675,800	Proprietary
Product	Bookseller Publication Catalog $0.5 Mil.	PUBCAT	1,625,400	SQL Server
Product	Preferred Recordings $0.1 Mil.	PRCRDZ	200,300	MS Access

Figure 8–2 A part of CDCo data inventory.

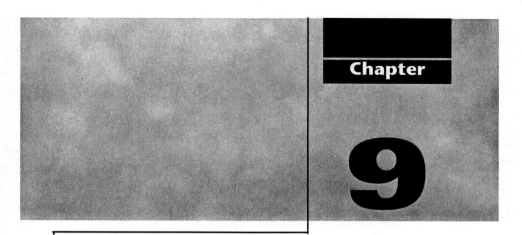

The Toolkit IT Framework: Standards

By the time we have taken the IT architecture from developing the principles to setting the standards, we have moved from the very conceptual to the fairly specific. Setting standards is one of the most detailed (and last) tasks performed by the architect in terms of setting direction for development.

The Toolkit definition of a standard is the agreed-to or corporate set of key data entities, functions, technologies, or processes—their names, definition, or description. We think it is very important for the architect to *set key standards* because standards serve as another step in translating the business view for developers.

Ground Rules for Setting Standards

Here are the fundamental decisions we recommend making as you set standards.

- Establish ownership.
- Define the state.
- Define the environment.
- Define the level of detail.

Establish Ownership

While it may seem counterintuitive, we believe that the architect—working closely with the business—should be responsible for setting standardized names and definitions for critical data and functions. This is because we have found that, when the business is involved in setting standards, those standards seem to have more *clout* and value. Standardized names chosen by developers may be very precise, but they may be confusing or irrelevant to the business. We recommend, therefore, that standard names and definitions reflect business terminology and use (e.g., Client versus Customer, Target Customers versus Marketing). Either the architect or the business spokesperson is a good candidate for ownership of standards.

Define the State

In most cases we would only spend time on setting standards for target-state components. Where feasible, you can maintain a translation of current to target state mappings in your repository.

Define the Environment

It is generally a good idea to begin with putting standards in place for the execution environment, then moving on to set standards for the operations environment. We recommend attacking the development environment last so that it can capitalize on standards already set for both the execution and operations environments.

Define the Level of Detail

I recommend treating setting standards as a decomposition of the Level n target state architecture model or of the target state inventory. When you use the architecture model as the basis for setting standards, you can use the function name and the associated proposed process name, role, and technology as the foundation for selecting which functions, processes, and technologies require standards. Similarly, the lowest-level architecture model (or conceptual data model)—which includes mega-entity names and proposed technology—can likewise be used to determine which data and technology require standards. When using a target state inventory as the basis for setting standards, key properties (like *name* in Figure 8–2) point you to the data, functions, processes, and technologies that require standards.

The following are some examples of standards for CDCo:

- *Function standard*   Target Customers—the function required to match current and prospective customer names, contact information (specifics here, such as email address), and demographic data from selected sources (specify them) with products and offers for the purpose of soliciting sales.
- *Technology standard*   As of January 2001, any new database will be created in Oracle on (platform). Existing files and databases will be examined for exception (*grandfathering*) or conversion.

Setting Function/Application Standards

When you are setting function standards, it is not only important to standardize the name and meaning/description of the function, but to cover other ground as well. The following are a couple of decisions you might want to consider while setting function standards.

- *Type/Priority of function*   For the most mission-critical functions, you may want to create (if you have not already done so) or strictly adhere to a set of development patterns (see Appendix D). This requires that, as part of setting the standard for each mission-critical function, you consider certain function characteristics (e.g., a high-volume, transaction-intensive function).

- *Candidate for migration to target*   Based on the priority, complexity, age, impact of change, and redundancy of existing applications that provide this function, you may want to earmark this function for early migration, consolidation, retention-as-is, etc., as part of the function standard.

Selecting Technology Standards

You may already have a process in place for selecting standard technology. If you do not, here is a basic approach we have used to evaluate and select technology for standardization.

1. Identify the types of components to be measured/evaluated, such as:
   - Operating System
   - RDBMS
   - Programming Language
   - Middleware
   - GUI

2. Define and describe selection criteria, such as the following:
   Fail-Safe
   - Backup and recovery
   - Disaster recovery
   - Monitoring/warning systems
   - Performance reliability

Scalability
- Time to add more processing power
- Cost to add more processing power
- Ease of adding more processing power

3. Define the measurement scale. We like to use a behaviorally anchored rating scale (BARS). This scale describes the behavior, characteristic, or function that an assigned numeric value represents. For example:
   - 4 = Provides complete capability
   - 3 = Provides most (75 percent or better) capability
   - 2 = Provides some capability (35–75 percent) capability
   - 1 = Provides little capability (< 35 percent) capability
   - 0 = Provides no capability

4. Rate each component against the BAR Scale, as show in Table 9–1.
5. Summarize findings for management, as shown below.

Operating System	Score
ABC	54 ◄——— **Winner!**
XYZ	40

As you are creating standards, bear in mind that you are at the appropriate place to begin to describe the *how* of the strategies you defined while developing architecture models. For example, if you created a messaging strategy, this would be the right place to name the messaging software you want to standardize and any rules for the construction of standard messages.

Setting People Standards

There are many facets of the "people side" of architecture—roles, skills, performance criteria, etc. When we get to later chapters, we will look at some of these factors in more depth. We will only mention people standards here. If we had to focus on one area to standardize, it

Table 9–1   Behaviorally Anchored Rating Scale (BARS)

| | OPERATING SYSTEM | |
	ABC	XYZ
Time to Market		
Startup Time for People (Learning Curve)	4	3
Resource (People) Availability	4	3
Startup Time For Hardware/Software (Order/Delivery)	4	3
Time to Change/Upgrade Code	4	3
Load Balancing		
Ability to Shift Resources across Functions	4	3
Ability to Maintain Response Time	4	2
Speed of Resource Reallocation	4	3
Fail-Safe		
Backup & Recovery	4	3
Disaster Recovery	3	3
Monitoring/Warning Systems	4	2
Performance Reliability	4	3
Scalabililty		
Time to Add More Processing Power	4	3
Cost to Add More Processing Power	3	3
Ease of Adding More Processing Power	4	3

would be identifying the critical skills and experience required to fill a specific IT role at a specific performance level.

Associate Data Architect at CDCo requires:

- Knowledge of
  - Information technology capabilities and trends
  - CDCo data assets

- CDCo of business functions
- CDCo current state architecture and strategies
- Skills
  - Extensive data analysis and modeling experience and proven skill
  - Proficiency with data analysis tools
  - Design experience in ODS, DIS—DW, or DM
  - Technical consulting skills and oral and written communications skills
  - BA/BS degree in IT or related field or equivalent experience

Setting Data Standards

This section could also be called *Why Intelligence is a Good Quality in People and a Poor Quality in Identifiers.* In case you thought we forgot about *data standards*, here is a longer commercial break: We believe that the mega- or key-entity identifiers are among the most important standards an architect can set—at least as important as technology standards! While most identifiers and other attribute standards will be established by the data analysts, we believe it is critical for architects to take the lead in setting the few core business identifier standards (Customer, Product, etc.). The definition of key concepts by the architect will serve to ensure the accurate translation of business intent and provide clear direction to data analysts.

The Good

Information technology pervades virtually every facet of our lives. New technologies have proliferated. Better architecture methods and rules-based solutions continue to improve how we approach constructing software. And yet, in many cases, we have not seen the corresponding improvement in time-to-market and software productivity that we ought to expect.

We hope that adopting new paradigms like e-business, Enterprise Application Integration (EAI), and Customer Relationship Management

(CRM) will solve our problems, make us more competitive, and give us the edge. We believe that XML and Metadata will save us. Unless we put the *information* back in IT, however, we will not realize the potential benefits of the brave new world of computing.

One common cause (in addition to the absence or insufficiency of architecture) of this apparent stagnation of progress is a lack of discipline regarding our data. Unless we clearly focus our energies on the data that is still at the heart of all our business solutions—e-business included—we will not see much improvement. And the key data area we need to address is the construction of good identifiers (no pun intended). Most architecture frameworks (ours included) require that we set data standards. The implementation of good data standards—especially for identifiers implemented as primary keys—can have tremendous impact. The *good identifier* can:

- Support resilience to change;
- Enable improved communication (e.g., across companies or partners); and
- Increase the speed of software delivery.

The Bad

Establishing good identifiers is critical in positioning us to take advantage of technological advances. How does a bad data standard separate us from good technology? Data is the message in any communication. If the message is muddled, unclear, or inaccurate, the quality of the communication is impaired—sometimes critically. Two partnering businesses, for example, communicate about their shared customers through EAI. If they speak to each other through translations of their respective customer identifiers, and those identifiers are not able to do their jobs, the result may be poor or no communication (e.g., no match).

What makes an identifier standard bad or good? A classic example of a bad identifier is a social security number (SSN). Even before there were laws that limited accessibility to SSNs, it was a flawed candidate for use as an employee identifier, for at least the following four reasons.

- It is not guaranteed unique and therefore not *persistent*.
- It contains intelligence and/or the intelligence is positional.
- It has limited capacity.
- An external party (i.e., the U.S. government) owns it.

The Ugly

1. An attribute(s) is not a good choice as a standard for an identifier if it is not guaranteed to be unique (and nearly unique is not good enough!). It is possible that an SSN can be reused. If it can be reused, then two people with the same name could be assigned the same SSN. The greater the number of occurrences, the greater becomes the possibility of incorrect identification. Potential duplicates, for example, can have a ruinous impact when dealing with thousands of employees—especially for key services like payroll and benefits administration (please give me back *my* paycheck!). It can also cause problems in identifying employees when they move between companies, as can happen due to an acquisition or a major outsourcing. Even when the numbers are not large, uniqueness is paramount in the selection of an identifier.

    Bottom Line   A good identifier needs to uniquely describe one, and only one, occurrence of an object.

2. A piece of data is not a good choice for an identifier if it contains intelligence. An identifier should uniquely describe a specific occurrence of an entity. If it is overloaded with *secret codes* and describes characteristics or relationships of that entity, and those characteristics or relationships change, the identifier will change. If I am identified by name and address, for example, and my address changes (which it has frequently), then every time I move, my identifier changes and the business cannot track me across addresses.

    Consider the structure of the standard United States telephone number. The North American Numbering Plan uses a structure of *NPA-NNX-NNNN*. NPA designates a region (area code), NNX designates a switch exchange, and NNNN designates a unique number within that exchange. The first three digits mean *geographic area* (positional intelligence). Sometimes, one of the three positions carries additional meaning (e.g., 0 or 1 in the middle position formerly meant *Phone Company Use Only*). Many lines of code have been written to translate which ten-digit code: a) is a real telephone number and therefore identifies a customer, b) has special meaning (describes how the call is billed, for example) or c) is reserved. Every time the meaning of one position changes, it can cause hundreds of thousands of instances across multiple (hundreds?) of tables to be affected and wreak havoc with the application code designed to interpret the number.

Bottom Line   A good identifier describes *which one* rather than *what kind it is* or *what we shall do with it*.

3. A field of data is not a good choice for an identifier when it is limited in its capacity to expand. A SSN is actually three pieces of data (nnn-nn-nnnn), and was not built to accommodate a world populated by billions of people. Furthermore, there is intelligence in an SSN (e.g., the middle two positions are related to year).

A telephone number is also not a good choice for a customer identifier—not only because it contains intelligence, but because it has a limited capacity. When a region (NPA) assigns the use of every available seven-position telephone number (NNX-NNNN), a new region is created to generate more available telephone numbers. The old NPA is split into old and new NPAs. All the customer information associated with the old NPA must be connected to the information associated with the new NPA. This means millions of values filling hundreds of tables across scores of companies must be relinked to the correct customer.

Bottom Line   A good identifier has plenty of room to accommodate orders of magnitude of expanded entries.

4. Any data element is not a good choice for an identifier if it is owned and controlled by an external entity. I still remember a discussion about the use of SSN as an employee identifier.

I asked how it would accommodate foreign-national employees. The other party proposed that we could replace the first character of the SSN with a (secret) letter code that would allow identification of foreign-national employees. After I explained that this was a bad idea (compounds the nonuniqueness, adds more intelligence, and further limits already limited capacity), I pointed out that even if this were a good idea, we do not control SSNs. We do not assign them, we cannot track their use, nor can we change them. And, heaven forbid, if the United States government decides to change the SSN format (i.e., develops a new scheme or expands the old one), all of our tables and applications that deal with employees will be affected!

Bottom Line   A good identifier is owned and managed by the organization using it.

The Payoff

We are big proponent of using nonintelligent, or *natural*, identifiers. Good examples of nonintelligent identifiers are:

- Sequentially assigned, purely numeric data, like *badge numbers* for employee identifiers;
- Randomly generated alpha/numeric code (e.g., as a customer identifier); and
- A natural identifier (e.g., the sequential order number on a preprinted order form).

The following are several reasons why the use of nonintelligent and natural identifiers helps create a business advantage:

- *Resilience*   When the business changes, a good identifier can support the change. For example, when a company doubles in size because of a merger or the acquisition of another business, it is not necessary to establish a new employee identifier. The scheme used has no hidden meaning and has the capacity to grow. Nor is there a need to clean up the data before the completion of the merger (e.g., we do not have to figure out which existing employees are duplicates because the identifier is guaranteed to be unique).

- *Improved Communication*   If the business acquires a partner that has its own list of similar products, we may be able to add them to our product table (because the identifier has no hidden meaning, plenty of capacity, and we control it). It may also be preferable to communicate about products with the new partner through messaging or some other form of EAI. With most legacy applications, data translation/mapping is the most complex project to complete in order to enable EAI. If the product identifier is unique, nonintelligent, and under our control, it will not "take a village" to decode and translate the product identifiers to a common language.

- *Time-to-Market*   When, for example, the organization has decided to sell services through the Internet, we can get the Web sales application up quickly if we can access and use the existing customer and product tables. We do not have to develop a separate Web customer table or create a new identifier (e.g., email address) even though there is new information. In fact, using an email address as a customer identifier for Web-based sales is a bad idea and would soon slow us down (more than one person can use the same email address, and the same person can have more than one email address, etc.). If CRM is a priority, adding the email address relationship to an existing customer data structure can enhance knowledge of the customer. In fact, it is very difficult to implement a CRM approach unless we can very clearly identify the "C" in CRM. Good identifiers actually promote reuse!

Then and Now

Finally, I need to confess that when I was a programmer, it was actually laudable to cram as much information as possible into as few bytes as possible. In fact, the programmer who developed the trickiest code set won the most respect. This even made sense when coding for a CPU with 16K!

Today's technologies have removed almost every constraint from data processing—size, speed, space, and location. It is now possible to focus on the most important actions we need to take to enjoy the benefits of these advances—ensuring the best possible data becomes reliable business information. The thoughtful creation and implementation of *good* identifiers can help the business go the distance today and into the future.

Some Good Examples

Here are some examples of the types of data that may be forgotten or overlooked when it comes to setting data standards. Because they are often foundation or building-block types of data, and often easy to standardize, it is especially important to set *good* standards for those.

- *Model Data*   A product model is an example of this. A product model describes the specification for a physical item that the corporation may want to include in an offer and wants to track. Each product model ought to be identified by a *product model number* associated with it (potential key) and is characterized by physical attributes such as size, weight, material, and available colors. Examples of product models are: Nokia Model xyz cell phone, AT&T Model 7406+ desk phone.

- *Instance Data*   A product instance is an example of this. A product instance describes a specific occurrence of a product model and typically has a serial number associated with it. A product instance describes a unique physical occurrence of an implemented product model (e.g., the color of the product model with this serial number). An example of a product instance is: My blue AT&T Model 7406+ desk phone, serial # 94sp55312298 can be identified by (*Product Model No., Product Serial No*).

- *Type Data*   A service type is an example of this. A service type describes a basic functional capability. In telephony, for example, a communications service type might include such occurrences as voice telephony, data facsimile transmission, Internet access, audio/visual data transmission, voice messaging, text messaging, etc., and could be identified by (*Communications Service Type ID*).

Suggested Exercise

Based on all the work you have done so far, list the top ten mega-entities (identifiers) you would standardize. List several identifiers you would expect the data analysts to define.

Integration—Again

As you have probably guessed, integration across architecture outputs is a key theme for us. We have already looked at how outputs that are created using the business framework are related to outputs that are created using the architecture framework. Figure 9–2 illustrates how outputs created within the architecture framework are related to each other.

By following the process (see Figure 9–1) we just described in the architecture framework, you will translate a set of target business opportunities to IT architecture. You will also expand the audit trail—the set of linked business and architecture outputs that describe how you arrived at this destination. We emphasize this because it will allow you to find, analyze, and track architecture change against business change. Finally, you will have created a sound foundation for data modeling and design, application design or selection, and technology implementation.

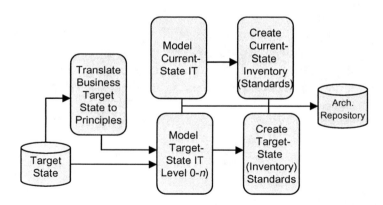

Figure 9–1   Toolkit process flow—IT framework.

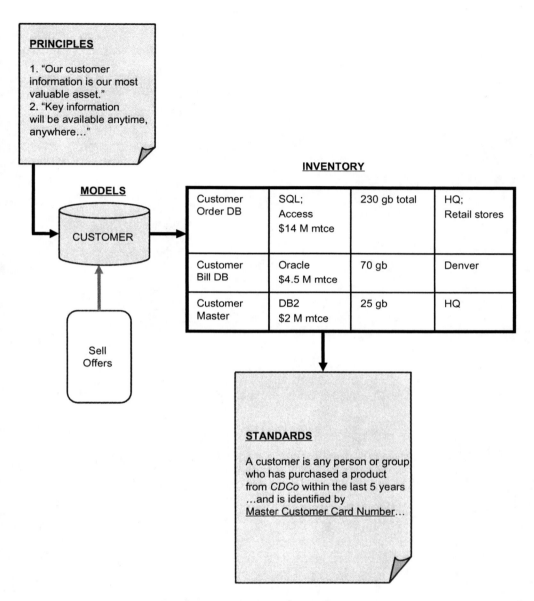

PRINCIPLES

1. "Our customer information is our most valuable asset."
2. "Key information will be available anytime, anywhere…"

MODELS

CUSTOMER

Sell Offers

INVENTORY

Customer Order DB	SQL; Access $14 M mtce	230 gb total	HQ; Retail stores
Customer Bill DB	Oracle $4.5 M mtce	70 gb	Denver
Customer Master	DB2 $2 M mtce	25 gb	HQ

STANDARDS

A customer is any person or group who has purchased a product from *CDCo* within the last 5 years …and is identified by Master Customer Card Number…

Figure 9–2 Putting it together—IT framework relationships.

The Toolkit Framework for Implementation: Projects

As difficult as it may be to create enterprise architecture, it may be more difficult still to move from architecture to implementation. We continue to find that efforts to build, manage, and use enterprise IT solutions often fail. Meanwhile, if there is one truth you can rely on, it is that the business of the business will keep shifting, and even if large undertakings reach completion, they may no longer be relevant. The following are some key, often-repeated mistakes that we believe contribute to the failure of enterprise IT solutions:

- Attempts to implement too much, too quickly
- Inability or lack of willingness to tie implementation to business success
- Underestimation of resistance to change
- No commitment and/or buy-in from the entire organization
- Lack of supporting enterprise-wide processes
- Insufficient focus on the people issues

The Framework for Implementation

So the third leg of our Toolkit focuses on a set of implementation strategies designed to address and mitigate these problems. Our framework for implementation is illustrated in Figure 10–1.

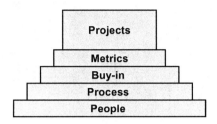

Figure 10–1   Framework for implementation.

Translating Architecture to Projects

The first block in our set of implementation strategies focuses on translating the architecture to projects. In most organizations, the best way to begin to realize the target is through small, easily implemented projects that are clearly linked to solving business problems. Here are the practical steps we take for overcoming the urge to implement too much at once:

1. Identify candidate projects (translate the architecture into business-focused projects)

2. Select/prioritize key projects

3. Narrow the scope of selected projects

Rather than an all-or-nothing approach, our prescription is to enable implementation of the target architecture by defining very small projects. Actualizing the target architecture through small, pragmatic projects beats trying to get the organization to swallow the architecture whole! So we approach implementation by defining easily implemented architecture projects, which address business gaps, solve business problems, or actualize business opportunities. We are looking for those projects best suited for early implementation. We want to be successful while delivering business benefit so we can have the opportunity to prove the real value of architecture to the business.

Not every project is an architecture project. By "architecture project" we mean a project that meets the following criteria.

- It is a discrete, well-scoped set of IT tasks (specific action[s] performed on specific data).
- It has a well-defined business output (meets a business need identified using the business framework).
- It can (and will!) be delivered within a short (e.g., three month) timeframe.
- It has an identified business sponsor/set of business user(s).
- It is likely to be funded (more later).
- It moves the IT infrastructure towards target—that is, the implementation is compliant with the target architecture.

We have had students ask how this definition gets us to a different set of projects than we might have developed using intuition, or than the organization's annual plan might have defined. The difference lies in the last part of the description and relates to what is implemented and how it is implemented. In other words, it is an architecture project if it implements or begins to implement a target state data store, function, service, or technology without requiring future rework.

Identifying Architecture Projects

Our first step in getting to a small, realistic set of architecture projects is to identify major, critical *potential* projects. We do this by examining the gaps and opportunities we articulated using the business framework. We then look at how we translated gaps and opportunities to target architecture components. The following details how to identify candidates for architecture projects.

1. Begin by examining *opportunities* for potential projects. Then translate the gap or opportunity into a statement that describes a project. The following are examples.
   - *Target state*   Customers can order any combination of products.
   - *Gap*   CDCo cannot process combination orders
   - *Opportunity*   Sell *combo offers* that include music, books, rewards, and/or new products
   - *Potential Project*   Build the capability to sell combo offers
2. Then, locate and extract the architecture components that result from the opportunity. The architecture models you create are often the easiest source of architecture components. Draft a rough *project scope* by listing the set of minimally required infrastructure components. For example, in Figure 7–6 (*CDCo Level 0 Target State Architecture Model*), the potential project "Build the Capability to Sell Combo Orders" required a few new/modified infrastructure components. Each one of the following might be a project:
   - *Datastores*   CDCo and Bookseller Product data stores, Combo Offer data store
   - *Functions*   A function that creates offers, a function that accesses offers, and a new/modified function that handles the ordering of offers
   - *Architecture service*   User interface for sales and ordering
   - *Data flow*   Linkage to legacy applications

Here is another example from CDCo.

1. Translate the opportunity to a project statement.
   - Target   Complete and accurate knowledge of customer characteristics and preferences improves marketing and sales results
   - *Gaps*   Customer data is not all automated or accessible to marketing; information is not aggregated centrally or easily available

- *Opportunity* Centralize key customer data; enable marketing access

- *Potential Project* Consolidate CDCo and Bookseller customer card history data to improve targeted marketing

2. Extract the architecture components.

   Here are the new/modified architecture components for this potential project. As in the previous example, delivering each of these components, or the combination of a couple, might constitute an architecture project:

   - *Service* User interface (Web portal) for marketing to access customer data

   - *Data* Common customer table

   - *Function* CRM/analytics for targeting, segmenting customers

While this method of identifying potential architecture projects may seem tedious, remember that we are focused on explicitly maintaining the business connection at every step of output creation.

There are other methods we can use to identify potential projects from the target architecture. If you are having trouble identifying architecture projects by examining opportunities and target state models, try one of the following methods.

- Continue modeling. Perhaps you have not decomposed the architecture sufficiently. You can model the next level of current state architecture to identify a more discrete problem, or you can model the next level of target state architecture to identify a more discrete solution (new/modified component).

  If you completed a Level 1 target state model, for example, you can see what proposed solution is exposed in the Level 2 target state model (e.g., a new data store, a new function, or a new architecture service).

- Examine the inventory for glaring duplicates, omissions (e.g., 24-order applications, no offer data store). This sort of review can help to identify projects with expense reduction or revenue potential.

In either case, make sure the candidate project directly supports or enables a primary business opportunity you identified using the business framework.

CDCo/Bookseller Candidate Y2000 Projects

The following is the list of potential projects we developed for CDCo using these approaches.

1. *Build Combo Offers*   Create an offer table with valid offers and pricing that links CDCo, Bookseller, and reward products to combo offers to support combined e-sales.

2. *Consolidate CDCo and Bookseller Customer Data*   Build the Customer Cross-reference table and assign the cross-organization Customer Number identifier to support CRM.

3. *Consolidate websites*   Move CDCo software and staff into Bookseller infrastructure; create Web access to Combo Offer and Customer data tables to improve sales.

4. *Upgrade e-Customer Service*   Begin implementation of CRM in the call center by automating e-customer Service Problem data and provide status reports to e-customers.

5. *Build Customer Data Warehouse*   Begin to consolidate CDCo and Bookseller customer card history data in a Customer data warehouse and build analytics for marketing targeting.

6. *Integrate Employee Information*   Assign a common Badge Number identifier to all CDCo and Bookseller employees to improve the matching of employees to work locations.

7. *Improve Training Information*   Organize Employee data store for access/search by Job and Skill codes to support cross-training.

8. *Consolidate Financials*   Migrate budget and reconciliation functions from spreadsheet to database to enable cross-organization financial reporting.

9. *Improve Order Flow/Develop EAI Strategy*   Apply EAI business process automation tool for order process flow to optimize order integration/costs of legacy applications.

Selecting Architecture Projects

The next sections discuss how to select and refine the scope of candidate projects you have identified. They are included because we have learned repeatedly that "good things come in small packages." I have been far more successful in gaining funding and support for a few key projects than by proposing to cure all the organization's ills with one giant pill (in fact, this often led to me being viewed as one giant pill).

Therefore, we now want to set about selecting a small, actionable subset of projects from the complete list of candidates. The following are some approaches that have worked for us.

Estimate Project Resources

There is no sense in proposing a $40 million project to a business that wants to spend a total of $20 million on all its IT infrastructure projects. Get help from the development organization to estimate, at a gross level of detail, the time and cost required to implement key projects. How can an architect tell if it is a $40 million project? We have used the following logic at a high level to estimate (and often eliminate) potential projects based on work effort.

- A wording change to an existing call center script, or adding a value to an existing table should take hours (if not, you may want to look at your administrative processes).
- A single, consolidated database can take years to build.

Appendix E shows a detailed example and the rationale we have used for constructing high-level estimates of work effort in large, complex organizations. We used this approach to estimate the proposed project time and effort for CDCo. This was not intended to be a highly scientific estimate, but rather an order-of-magnitude estimate to help us eliminate projects that were clearly too large to undertake as *first steps*. These too-large projects may be highly critical to the organization's success, so this type of exercise also points you to very important architecture projects that may require further decomposition or chunking up before they can realistically be undertaken. It is the approximate sizing—applied consistently—rather than the method that is important, so you can feel free to develop a different sort of scale that may be better suited to your environment.

Another approach to dealing with the time and cost issues surrounding the funding of projects is to brush up on your skills of persuasion. In some cases we have been convinced that the extra funding needed to implement a very large, but essential, piece of infrastructure has such tremendous business benefit that, rather than eliminate a large project because of its size, we will *sell* the business using the "pay now and save later" kind of logic, as shown in the following list.

- Build this table now because additions to tables are simpler, faster, and less expensive than changes to code. Standard tables for offers, products, and customers can ease the addition of new partners or products.
- Build this single-purpose function now because multipurpose functions require more and more complex code changes to add new features. Single-purpose functions (e.g., Calculate Bill, Create Journal Entry) coupled with access to standard tables enable time-to-market and competitive advantage when implementing new concepts.
- Implement standard messages now because creating multiple and/or new pair-wise interfaces between functions is time consuming and often inaccurate. The use of standard messages (e.g., order message) saves time, money, and misunderstandings.
- Fund this one architecture-aligned project rather than multiple, competing nonarchitected projects because parallel project-focused efforts cause duplicate infrastructures to be built and—more expensively—maintained (cost of multiple fix-up projects versus a well-built single-purpose piece of architecture).
- This is a good investment (it takes money to make money) because building basic IT infrastructure components—single-purpose functions, like the creation of tables and messages—require investment but return dollars, flexibility, and time-to-market improvements.

Prioritize Projects

If you have a very long list of candidate projects, you may want to select or eliminate some by using multivoting, or some other statistical or standard quality improvement methodology. If you use voting to prioritize, participants having a vote should be recognized experts—perhaps a member of your architecture governing board or steering committee (more about this when we talk about architecture governance). You should then develop a scale to gauge priority. As discussed in Chapter 2, for example, many organizations have a widely publicized list of a few key goals or drivers. You can apply points for each goal or driver satisfied by each candidate project,or you can develop a BARS (see Chapter 9) to measure the extent to which each project enables the goal or driver. We generally use a four-point scale since it has no mid-range value (too easy an out). For project prioritization, our scale might look something like this:

4 = Project is pivotal to achievement of goal

3 = Project supports goal

2 = Project minimally supports or does not hamper goal

1 = Project has no impact or adverse impact on goal

Projects that receive the most points remain on the *Selected Projects* list. This usually requires defining a cutoff point, because you will not have accomplished much by selecting 98 of the 100 proposed projects. We often set a limit in advance of the vote (e.g., top ten or fifteen projects) or we look for natural break points (significant jump in point value from one project to the next) in the tally that results from the vote. Using a systematic voting process not only helps to eliminate conflict around pet projects, but also contributes to the audit ability of your architecture effort.

Data-Driven Approach to Project Selection

By now you may suspect that we are data bigots. That is because—having approached architecture from almost every angle—we remain persuaded that going after common data is a sound approach that can deliver broad benefit. When we take a data-driven approach to selecting projects, we:

- Identify key data areas; and
- Apply prioritization criteria.

We often use a particular data-driven approach to selecting and scoping projects. Today's enterprise has become more distributed via partnerships, mergers, e-business, and outsourcing. We advocate applying the driving business strategy (e.g., *partnerships and distribution*) to implementing architecture. This means, for example, that if the organization is in the process of distributing work or functions to partners and keeping few functions centralized, then you might want to consider distributing associated data and keeping only a very little common data centralized. If, on the other hand, your organization is focused on consolidating work or functions, you may want to consider collapsing relevant data.

To determine key pieces of architecture to implement, our approach focuses on the target architecture—*key data areas*—to provide a map for selecting the few projects that implement "partnerships and distribution" or "consolidation." To do this, use the following steps.

1. Identify key data areas (often the same as mega-entities—see Chapter 7).

    - Extract the nonatomic sets of data (mega-entities like Customer and Offer) from the lowest-level target architecture model or conceptual data model.

    - List the key business opportunities collected in the business target state description (e.g., leverage the combined music/publications product lines).

    - List the candidate projects.

2. Map candidate projects to key data areas and key opportunities. These might be the same as the "few key drivers or goals" we mentioned previously.

3. Select a subset of the candidate projects based on the frequency of their intersection with key data areas and business opportunities, as depicted in Figure 10–2. This is really an extension of the prioritization approach we discussed earlier. The CDCo Level 0 Target State architecture model key data areas, for example, include Offer, Customer, and Order. Projects 1, 2, 3, and 4 have the highest frequency of intersection with each data area and the business drivers. Focus on high-frequency intersections of projects with data and business drivers.

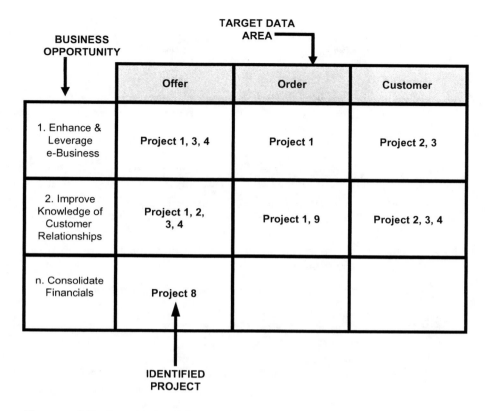

Figure 10–2   The CDCo project selection matrix.

Apply Viability Criteria

These are the criteria we recommend you apply to select the final list of projects. If a project does not meet all of the viability criteria, it may not be an appropriate project for early implementation. We zero in on projects that:

- Are manageable in scope (able to be delivered in realistically short time frames);
- Deliver business benefit for each project (or subproject) implementation;

- Address a business gap, solve an identified business problem, and/or actualize a business opportunity (see business framework);
- Do not create *throwaway* solutions;
- Support flexibility (e.g., reuse) and affordability; and
- Allow for, or contribute to, phased migration to target information architecture.

For example, we considered Candidate Project #5: Build (CDCo and Bookseller) Customer Data Warehouse. This project was not manageable in scope and would not allow for phased migration to target architecture. An alternative proposal—Prototype Customer Data Warehouse—might constitute a viable substitute, whereas Candidate Project #4 (Upgrade e-Customer Service) appears to be manageable in scope and allows for a phased migration to the target.

Hint	We strongly suggest that when you have developed a list of selected projects, you give each project a short name (i.e., verb+noun—for example "Build Combo Offers"). When you skip this step, others (e.g., executives, project managers) will tend to do this for you. The names they choose often convey something other than what you are proposing. Not surprisingly, this can lead to missed expectations, or at least confusion.

Suggested Exercise

Create a list of candidate projects.

Six Strategies for Containing Project Scope

When we have selected the projects we believe make the most sense to implement, we then intentionally *further limit the scope* of each project. We do this for several reasons.

- Smaller projects incur less risk.
- Smaller projects require fewer resources.

- Smaller projects are more likely to be successfully implemented, and success breeds success (and often, more funding).

- *Scope-creep* (the tendency of every IT project to expand its boundaries far and wide) seems almost inevitable, so why not head it off?

Because we are sure you will figure it out, we will tell you up front that our strategies for refining project selection and minimizing project scope are also data-centric. Our basic strategy is to identify *scoped* subsets of target architecture data stores/functions that can be made available and useful in a short timeframe. This is loosely based on the business strategy we referred to earlier—minimal centralization and more distribution (e.g., via partnerships, mergers, e-business and outsourcing). The de-scoping strategies we use apply the *business strategy*—applying "minimal centralization and more distribution"—to implementing architecture. We create communication across the infrastructure data and applications (legacy, partners, and the Web) through messaging or key cross-reference tables. We allow most data to remain distributed (legacy, partner, etc.).

The following sections detail the six strategies we use for containing project scope.

First Things First

Historically, we attempted to consolidate all the same data from different partners or sources into a single data store. This often (always?) failed.

Undertaking *First Things First* means beginning data integration via linking or cross-referencing of the same data identifiers. This strategy focuses on implementing and matching identifiers prior to, or instead of, wholesale data mapping and consolidation. Here is how it works:

- Establish a common or master identifier (e.g., Master Product Code—see "Setting Data Standards")

- Relate other existing identifiers (e.g., from legacy systems or partners) to the master identifier through messaging, XML tags, or a cross-reference table

For example, CDCo acquired Bookseller because it wants to sell both product lines to customers of both companies. Each company identifies the customer differently. Messaging or cross-referencing both customer identifiers to the Master Customer Identifier allows both parties to easily understand who is placing an order.

The business payoff for this approach is that it provides immediate integration benefits to the enterprise, which is critical even if we never get to later steps. It provides the ability to find all customers by any known identifier while allowing for later data consolidation.

Use It or Lose It

We used to concentrate on collecting and modeling all the attributes of the data and getting it right before undertaking data implementation. The only problem with this approach is that it seems we are never finished with data modeling. Use it or lose it suggests that it is more important to collect, model, and store a vital (new) attribute and have a parallel plan for immediate availability of that data. In other words, you must:

- Select the most critical piece(s) of data and implement; and
- Create easy access to this data (e.g., API, message distribution, or even a report) as part of the project plan.

Like many companies, for example, CDCo quickly put up a website for customer ordering, and in the process of doing so, created new functions and new instances of Customer, Product, and Order tables. The new Customer table contains several e-attributes, including Email Address. The whole area of e-customer attributes has not been modeled or analyzed yet, but marketing is clamoring for email addresses. Capturing email addresses only and adding it to the Customer Cross-Reference table or a viable legacy customer table provides an additional valuable customer attribute for immediate use.

The business payoff here is that information is broadly (and quickly) available. Capturing data without deploying it can lead to problems. *When not used, data may lose its currency, or at least its credibility, and therefore its value.* This way, new strategic information is quickly available to the fulfillment, marketing, and sales departments and could be available to legacy systems through messaging or cross referencing.

No Data before Its Time

We repeatedly attempted to secure funds to implement all target data sets at once (because it is *right*!). This often only succeeded in having us removed from the discussion. *No data before its time* recommends focusing on implementing parts of target data that solve specific and urgent enterprise needs. Target data is built when there is a compelling business reason to do it. We still use the enterprise target architecture and the conceptual data model as the blueprints for the solutions.

- Capitalize on the timing of an urgent business project to subset data to be implemented (which increases the likelihood that the solutions will be funded).

For example, as the CDCo enterprise enters the Internet space, it becomes increasingly important to them to understand their customers' credit payment behavior. There is a great deal of existing credit data available in multiple CDCo databases, and there is a new target state model for credit management, but the most pressing need is to capture and store credit-scoring data. It would be expensive and time consuming to implement the target model in one chunk. CDCo, however, could quickly make one or more elements of credit data available in the customer tables.

The business payoff here is that critical information is available when the enterprise needs it, and the enterprise needs it now! This solution makes credit scores available to marketing and sales departments very quickly, and other parts of the model can be implemented as business priorities dictate.

Smaller Is Better

It always used to make sense to implement all the instances of the target data. Unfortunately, this might take a lifetime. *Smaller is Better* suggests creating a small subset of a target data store population and making it available in a critical area of the enterprise. This approach has the advantage of providing a subset of data that has immediate benefit and helps to build credibility (which may beget more funding). The focus is on creating manageable, deliverable chunks.

- Implement a specific population of the target data.

CDCo, for example, has found that online ordering has resulted in new service trouble-reporting demands on the existing infrastructure. CDCo does not have an up-to-date service problem tracking application and data store. Now that CDCo has expanded due to the purchase of Bookseller, the number of online orders is expected to grow exponentially. New orders are also more complicated (CD and book combinations). CDCo needs an order service problem-tracking data store. While it might eventually contain all order service problems, it would provide immediate benefit to the business to implement a subset of service problems (i.e., only those problems that occur and are reported by online customers).

The business payoff in this case is a new ability (handles e-business service problem resolution) to support the new enterprise target, *decoupled from every possible capability*. CDCo is also creating the ability to provide continuous enterprise benefit with each additional set of instances that is implemented.

Just in Time

We used to wait until all information about a transaction was complete before implementing an instance. We sometimes had partially processed transactions lying about for eons, however, until millions of them eventually fell into a black hole somewhere.

Just in time suggests that we ought to capture what information we know, when we know it in the process. Because many business problems are process problems, they often require many steps and a long duration to repair. With this strategy, we capture and store the data associated with each process step as the step is repaired, even when this leaves you with data *in progress*. In-progress data has a value of its own—it can provide key measurement information (e.g., are there always many more pending orders than complete orders, and if so, why?). This approach can actually help facilitate process change, while making some state of the target data available for analysis.

- Store data when it occurs in the enterprise process, instead of waiting for multiple, dependent events to complete (this one has the best potential to qualify as a radical heresy!).

For example, CDCo's new multipart customer order (e.g., books, CDs, and a free gift) requires complex, multiple events to fulfill. The early capture of customer information as we get it would allow us to better satisfy our customers' needs and manage our processes. So, when we have the first significant contact with a customer—perhaps an inquiry about a book—we create an occurrence of Customer. When the customer places a first order, we create an occurrence of Customer Account. When the order is submitted, we create an instance of Pending Customer Order. And we make the information immediately accessible (use it or lose it).

The business payoff is the availability of key data earlier in the process and better tracking of process gaps. Customer, account, and pending order information are available to marketing, sales, and service departments even before the order is fulfilled.

Something New under the Sun

Some of us (and here I include myself) may have been overly efficient by *overloading* existing data by adding new meaning to it. *Something new Under the Sun* requires isolating a new set of data to its own *tablet* so that it can be most useful to the enterprise. It also includes creating all the rules, processes, and messages required to implement the change. This is a case of enterprise change driving data change. We can look at a business change as an architecture *opportunity*. When a business change drives a funded project, it presents an opportunity for the architecture to decouple, or untangle, an existing knot. Usually, the fix is to:

- Build a new table for new data

For example, the original product code for CDCo was used to identify records. Over time, the product codes have been used to describe records, sheet music, audio and video tapes, DVDs, and CDs. In fact, one position of the product code was eventually used to describe the recording media (egads!).

Of course, the correct answer is "No!" The existing system infrastructure was not built to accommodate books, and neither was the identifier. When this kind of a change occurs, it is the right time to decouple by beginning to untangle existing *spaghetti* data.

The business payoff is that new information can clearly be located, tracked, and measured. This data decoupling also supports the capability to offer CD, book, and free gift combos—or any other new kind of product. An added benefit is also faster market entry for new offerings (table update versus code changes).

The following is an example of the way these steps—identifying candidate projects, selecting a subset of projects, and minimizing project scope—come together for CDCo.

- The candidate project, Build Combo Offers, is limited in scope to "Build the Combo Offers table, populate it with new (post-2000) offers, and allow online and call center access" (smaller is better). It does not result in a throwaway solution and allows for phased migration—other offers and channels can be added later.

- The candidate project, Upgrade e-Customer Service, has been limited to implementing only instances of problems that are reported online (smaller is better). This project is viable—manageable in scope and allows for phased migration. Even if you only implement this project, you will have addressed a business problem and begun to move to target.

- The candidate project, Consolidate CDCo and Bookseller Customer Data, has been limited by specifying that consolidation will begin by linking key existing customer identifiers (first things first).

The result of applying these strategies to target architecture candidate projects is set of smaller projects that provide the following benefits:

- Increased enterprise flexibility
- Better integration through wide distribution and use of key common data

- Increased accuracy through reconciliation of values for key attributes
- Postponement/elimination of costs associated with massive data consolidation efforts

The Project Brief

I know that I have confounded architecture teams when I have insisted they take this business of projects one step further. We strongly recommend that the architect take responsibility for at least the first, brief (no pun intended) description of the project. Having the architect describe each selected project clearly and succinctly supports on-target implementation. The following are some suggestions for how to accomplish that.

- Get help from your project management organization. Volunteer to support project management by creating a Statement of Work (SOW) for each project (and with any other handoff from architecture needed to facilitate the implementation plan).
- Create a condensed SOW for each project, if you are familiar with standard project management practices.
- Tailor a project description that suits your organization. At a minimum, the basic project description or *project brief* needs to include the following details.

  - *Why* Project business purpose or benefit (per business framework content)
  - *What* One or two statements that define the project
  - *Who* Project sponsor or owner
  - *When* High-level timeline or major milestones
  - *Where* Geographic scope or user base
  - *How* Constraints or limitations
  - *How much* Gross estimate of costs

The effort required to create a project brief is more than offset by the benefit of clearly communicating the intent and scope of the architecture project. The brief can also be very succinct. The following is an example of a basic project brief for the CDCo candidate project, Build Combo Offers.

Project Brief—Build Combo Offers

Business Opportunity Combination CDCo/Bookseller offers have great revenue potential.

Description This project creates an Offer table (including pricing) that links CDCo, Bookseller, and promotional gift products to support enhanced e-sales. This includes the following.

- *Data* Building Offer Cross-Reference table, analyzing and mapping products to offers, and populating tables with new (2000) offers.
- *Functionality* Building rules and access to offers. Modifying Web and call center screens, and building Create/Maintain Offer.
- *Platform Technology* MS Access for Offer table, MS Active Server pages.

Owner Marketing.

Users E-Combo offers will be available to U.S. customers and to all call center service reps (one U.S. location) via the common Web interface (where 35 percent of sales are expected to occur in 2000).

Estimated Time and Cost $100–120K for a team of four to deliver in 3.5 months.

Benefits

- Supports five percent improvement in revenue assigned to online and call center sales channels
- Supports marketplace change and flexibility to respond quickly with new offers

---

We will discuss interactions with other key groups in upcoming chapters, but I wanted to mention the *flexibility factor* here. I have always asked my architecture teams to create *nonarchitecture* outputs—from missing business or IT documents to SOWs for projects. I have required them to participate in, or support teams, in the creation of *any* other handoff from architecture that was needed to facilitate the implementation plan. The success of architecture is linked to the success of the project managers and all the other key players. So, in addition to perseverance, flexibility is a critical characteristic for the architect.

Suggested Exercise

From your list of candidate projects, select one or two and reduce the scope. Write a project brief.

Summary

Much of the work we have done to come up with a small set of truly viable projects lays the groundwork for us to develop metrics and gain concurrence for what we have determined to be the first set of key architecture projects.

11

The Toolkit Implementation Framework: Establishing Metrics

There continues to be a credibility gap in many IT organizations because the business perceives that IT fails to deliver, or the delivery does not meet expectations, or there is a lack of clear expectations. Coincident with this situation, we have also seen how difficult it often is to demonstrate the contribution of architecture to the success of the business. In this chapter we will look at some proven practices for assessing the effectiveness and value of architecture.

Measuring Architecture Effectiveness

One of the best ways to combat this kind of failure to demonstrate architecture value begins with establishing very clear expectations. The most tangible evidence of success or failure is frequently found at the project level. Was it implemented? Did it deliver what was needed? That is why we recommend assessing project success as one basis for

129

measurements—even some architecture measurements. Because linkage is so fundamental in our approach, we assess meeting the expectations for projects at the following three levels.

- Were the business objectives met?
- Were the project objectives met?
- Were the architecture objectives met?

In our lexicon, an objective is specific, measurable, and time-bounded. Here's an example of an objective that meets those criteria: "Reduce printing of duplicate customer bills to less than 1 percent by December 31, 2001." It is specific—"printing of customer bills." It is measurable—"less than 1 percent duplicated." And it is time-bounded—the result must be achieved by the stated date.

When we use projects as the basis for measurement, what are we really measuring?

- *Value—Business results*   What quantifiable benefit are we setting out to achieve for the enterprise?
- *Effectiveness—Project results*   To what extent was it delivered as promised (project objectives)?
- *Effectiveness—Architecture results*   To what extent does it operate in compliance with architecture (architecture objectives)?

When we discuss architecture governance in Chapter 13, we will cover an additional approach to measuring architecture compliance effectiveness by looking at *process measurements*.

Setting Business Objectives

Once again, we will begin with the business. We set business objectives for each project to measure the value of the project. To establish business metrics for architecture projects, review business framework analyses to determine the expected business benefit (e.g., why is this project being undertaken—to achieve an increase in revenue, or a reduction in expenses?). We stated earlier that a *viable* architecture project needed to address a specific business gap or an opportunity. So, we need to define a quantitative measure of positive change in the business, based on the specific gap or opportunity for each project. The specific objectives we use as measurements to guide the project and evaluate business success might be similar to: "Increase number of sales," or "Increase amount of revenue." If you cannot determine a measurement of positive change in the business, you may be working on the wrong project.

Here is an example from CDCo:

- *Opportunity*   Develop combo offers of book/music products
- *Project selected to address that opportunity*   Build Combo Offers
- *Metrics*
  - *Number of Sales*   By December 2000, sales of new combo offers through the Web channel will represent 10 percent of total sales.
  - *Amount of Revenue*   By December 31, 2000, combo offers sold via the Web will result in $5 million in revenue.

Setting Project Objectives

We set project objectives to measure the effectiveness of each project. To establish project metrics, use the project time, cost, and quality criteria included in the high-level project brief. For each criterion, define a quantitative measure of attainment. For example:

- *Criterion*   Populating tables with new (2000) Offers
- *Metric*   Tables populated

While on-time and within-budget delivery of the project are common measures, we advocate also including some quality measurements, which are often overlooked. Here are some project criteria for the Build Combo Offers project:

- *Estimated Time*   1st Quarter (delivered 3rd Quarter if funded by end of June 2000)
- *Users*   Begin implementation on the website and in the call center

The resulting metrics might be the following.

- *Complete, on time and within budget*   All new (in 2000) combo offers will be available in the Offer table by September 30, 2000, at a cost of no more than $110K.
- *Quality*   By December 2000, 90 percent of call center agents will be able to successfully process a combo offer order.
- *Quality*   By December 31, 2000, 80 percent of customer orders for combo offers will have no associated complaints of problems when ordered through the website (remember the business needs that led us to this project).

Setting Architecture Objectives

While establishing architecture measurements may seem amorphous, there are at least a few types of architecture measurements to consider putting in place. One approach is to set architecture objectives for each project to measure architecture effectiveness. To establish project-related architecture metrics, we need to examine what the expected outputs of architecture are for this project. What is architecture expected to contribute to project success? Some suggestions for our Build Combo Offers example might be the following.

- *Compliance*   The project design complies with 2000 target architecture (more about this when we discuss governance).
- *Completeness*   The architecture for Combo Offers is complete and reviewed with the project team by June 30, 2000.

Measuring Architecture Value

While project-related architecture measurements are very useful and even necessary, they are most likely insufficient for assessing the *value* that the architecture function provides to the business, or even why it is a good investment to staff an architecture team. To estimate the value provided by architecture, it is necessary to look at architecture from a different and broader perspective. One approach we have used involves the following:

- Collecting benchmark data
- Collecting sample performance data
- Applying benchmark estimates to the sample
- Projecting savings

The benchmark data we use is industry-collected data about the impact of architecture on the cost of IT. The sample performance data we use is the current cost of sample IT projects to the organization *without* a target architecture in place that is used as the basis for review of architecture compliance. What we are trying to quantify is the savings that can accrue from developing and maintaining an enterprise architecture, and then using that architecture as the basis for guiding a proposed project design so that it complies with the architecture. This assumes that "The purpose of enterprise architecture is to align the IT infrastructure with the organization in a way that best promotes the organization's goals, while maximizing the benefit of IT dollars spent."

Benchmark Data

The data below are examples of benchmark data used to measure the savings opportunity or impact of architecture on the cost of IT. This example is data cited by John Zachman, the "Father of Enterprise Architecture." When using a rigorous approach to architecture, one might expect to see:[1]

- Enterprise data handling labor reduced 50 percent
- Reduced development time of 25 percent through improved communication and conflict resolution
- Development time and cost reductions for every succeeding implementation of >50 percent, compounded through reuse of database and application components with no modifications

---

[1] From 10/25/01 "Framework for Enterprise Architecture, Enterprise Physics 101," referencing work of practitioners.

Here is another example of industry data, resulting from the use of improved data management methods and tools. These reflect individual case study results.[2]

- Increased ROI of 250 percent over three years
- Reduced data cycle time from twenty-two days to <twelve hours
- Two-percent profit increase
- Average (conservative) savings of 20 percent in IT costs
- Consolidation of databases from thirty-five to one

Like many advertisements for diet products, we want to state that these results may not be typical. They are anecdotal, but can be useful in terms of the kind of impact target architecture can have when used to govern development.

Sample Data

To determine the *current cost of projects* without a target architecture and compliance review process in place, we would select a sample of projects currently funded and underway (or just completed) in the organization. This might be ten or twenty projects, depending on the total number underway in the organization. Appendix F provides an example of a questionnaire we have used to collect sample data-centric project performance data, which works with the first benchmark we just cited. We collected at least the following information for each project:

- Total expenses for the project—Where possible, this can be further broken down by staff expense, software licenses, DASD, etc.
- Data costs as a percentage of the total expense (i.e., the costs associated with analyzing, designing, developing, and implementing new or modified tables and interfaces)
- Listing of significant, redundant data stores/interfaces

Figure 11–1 shows a case study—a sanitized version of actual data we collected in a complex, medium- to large-size organization, using a representative sample of projects of different sizes and characteristics. It illustrates a complete example of how this approach might work.

---

2. From "What Works?," case studies documented in *Data Warehousing*, v. 10.

PRO-JECTS	COSTS	DATA COST	KEY DATA	KEY INTERFACES	PROJ. BENEFITS
1.	$1.4 Mil. HC	25%	10 product data stores • 5 ODS • 5 DW	8 major data transfers • 4 External-daily • 4 ODS to DW-weekly	+ $90 Mil Rev. increase
2.	$0.5 Mil. HC	38%	4+ collections account data stores • ODS	7 major data transfers • 1 External-daily • 7 internal ODS-daily	- $1.5 Mil. Collections reduction
3.	$0.3 HC	75%	6 + account data stores • ODS	6 major data transfers • External to 6 ODS-daily	- $0.5 Mil. Risk reduction - $3. Mil. Collections reduction
4.	$0.4 Mil. HC	100%	6 account data stores • 5 ODS • 1 DW	5 major data transfers • 1 external to DW-weekly • 4 inter-ODS-daily	+ $05. Mil. Rev. increase
5.	$0.2 Mil. HC	30%	6 account data stores • ODS	5 major data transfers • 2 external to ODS-daily • 5 inter-ODS-daily	+ $15. Mil. Rev. increase
6.	$0.2 Mil. HC	50%	6 account data stores • ODS	6 major data transfers • 1 external to ODS-daily • 1 ODS to external-daily • 4 inter-ODS-daily	(Cost Avoid-ance)

Figure 11–1   Sample current-project performance data.

Calculating Savings Opportunity for Sample Data

Below is the method we used for calculating the opportunity for savings in the case study, based on the proposed improvements to the architecture practices. Since we wanted to be certain not to overestimate potential savings, our calculation was conservative—we selected a single benchmark factor that seemed to best fit what the organization planned to address.

```
Total project headcount expenses
X    Average: data-related percent of sample project's
headcount expense
X    Savings (using Zachman Benchmark, Factor #3)
_____
=    Savings opportunity for the sample projects
```

Even if we only use the sample projects in Figure 11–1, we can estimate some real savings using the following formula:

```
Six project HC expense = $3 milllion
X    Average percent data costs @ 50 percent = $1.5 million
(average = 53.6)
X    Zachman development cost reduction @ 50 percent
_____
=    $0.75 million opportunity (projected development time and
cost (HC) savings over next six projects with target
architecture and governance process in place)
```

Projecting Savings Opportunity

For many medium-to-large IT organizations with hundreds of projects annually, it would be reasonable to expect a savings opportunity of several millions of dollars in savings over a full year's worth of projects. To project the annual savings opportunity for the case study, for example, we would multiply the percent of average savings (50 percent average data costs × 50 percent cost reduction = 25 percent) by the annual project budget. Projections like these can be useful as part of the cost and benefit analysis for implementing an enterprise architecture function.

There are other approaches to measuring the value of architecture that work equally well. Depending on the organization's goals, you may find other benchmarks that are more appropriate. We have also used other data to make the case for architecture value. In one organization, constructing and presenting the current data inventory—with all its redundancy—helped secure architecture funding. In another organization, we counted the number of pair-wise (peer-to-peer) interfaces that existed in the current state architecture. This data was useful in making the business case for building some common architecture components.

We like our approaches because they are more concrete and practical than theoretical. What is most important is to take the time to collect the data to demonstrate the likely contribution of architecture. And because measurement is really an ongoing process, rather than a one-time event, the data would be evaluated over time to measure the actual contribution of architecture once you have put the new practices and processes in place.

Suggested Exercise

List one or two areas in your IT environment that would be good candidates for measurement. Consider both the availability of reliable data and stated organization goals.

The Toolkit Implementation Framework: Presenting the Plan for Buy-in

Even if your analysis is perfect and your outputs extraordinary, *it will be almost impossible* to implement your architecture unless you gain concurrence from key stakeholders. In our experience, more architecture implementations have failed because of politics than because of poor quality. When we say *politics*, we mean all the soft, cultural, and environmental interactions that occur between individuals and groups in your organization, especially around resistance to change. Successful communication in this arena is not only worth an investment of time, but it will directly enable buy-in to the architecture, as well. We believe it is vital to spend whatever time is required to gain agreement for the target architecture and the set of projects through which it begins to be implemented. Our goal goes beyond receiving head-nodding agreement. We are seeking active support for architecture. Do not be surprised if this takes a great deal of time (it once took me a year in an extremely large organization, but the payback was large for years to come) and try to remember that this is time well spent.

139

To succeed, whose buy-in or concurrence do you need? At a minimum, you must have support from the following groups:

- Business leadership
- IT leadership
- The CIO
- Development organization

Right now, you may be saying, "This is an architecture, not an election or a popularity contest!" But in many ways it is both. So, if you will humor us, we will look at some approaches that have been proven effective in winning supporters, if not converts, to your architecture. Some general advice includes the following.

- Publish or perish—Create a complete plan or architecture package for discussion and review with key stakeholders.
- Think about selling the architecture as you would any other effort needing funding.
- Reward participants, include everyone, and communicate everywhere!

Gaining Executive Support

In the Toolkit, the executive presentation is *required* to confirm architecture direction and to review and select key projects for *funding and implementation.*We include business leadership, IT leadership, and the CIO in this category. In your organization there may be other key opinion leaders you want to add. When you want to gain initial leadership support for the architecture, seek out and collect executive feedback before you begin and then throughout architecture development. Some "tried and true" techniques include the following.

- Schedule regular (e.g., quarterly), architecture reviews with the business leaders, the CIO, and IT department heads, or get organizational help to form a steering committee. In either forum, the more used to reading, reviewing, and discussing architecture outputs the executive team becomes, the less arcane and irrelevant they will appear.

- In addition, or if it is not feasible to schedule quarterly reviews, publish a brief quarterly architecture report for executive consumption and ask for feedback. Highlights are best (e.g., "The architecture website is up and working. Take a look at (URL) and give us feedback!").

- If it is rare to have the opportunity to make an executive architecture presentation, make the most of it. It should be interactive and memorable. (Also, while the fun and rewards need to be more sophisticated, officers are not immune to some *sugar* with their architecture *medicine*. We often include giveaways at these meetings.)

- Customize or scale down the architecture content.
  - Summarize the business needs/opportunities/gaps. You can abstract a brief synopsis from the business framework content you developed.
  - For the executive presentation it is most often necessary to construct a presentation-level model. The presentation model is constructed at an even higher level and is further abstracted than a Level 0 model.
  - For each business need, develop a brief proposal for the architecture solution (project). This should include text and model(s). Include benefits/proposed metrics even if they have not been fully quantified, and estimated time and cost for each proposed project. Project briefs can easily satisfy this need.
  - Develop a one-page *bottom line*—a prioritized summary of architecture projects, time, and cost.

Creating a Presentation-Level Architecture Model

A presentation-level model is an audience-specific, very conceptual abstraction of the Level 0 target state architecture model. Begin by mapping the Level 0 model functions, data stores, and services up one level. Only include technology where you seek funding to introduce it. A good rule of thumb is to construct an easily read and understood one-page model with around five to eight key functions and five to eight key data stores. The objective is to highlight the areas of the target where you want to focus immediate attention. We *do not recommend* showing the twenty-page current state applications and data architecture (a.k.a., *wiring diagram*) to every officer. Early on, we were so enthusiastic about our architecture outputs that we tried this—it did not work well! If you feel compelled to include your detailed architecture outputs, use them as appendices or backup data. Figure 12–1 shows an example of a presentation-level model for CDCo.

This is really a small piece of the target architecture abstracted into a partial presentation-level model. If this model succeeds in gaining funding and support for our top architecture projects, then it is the "right" model!

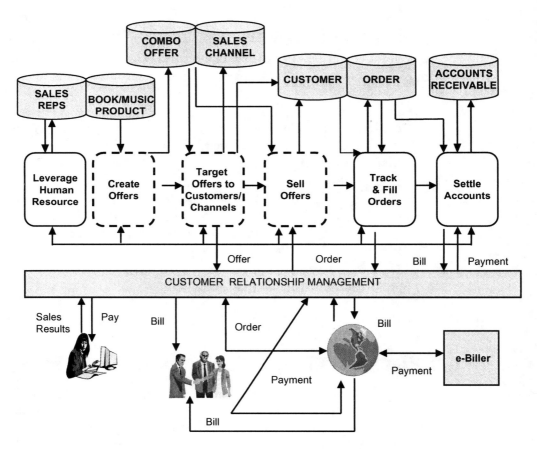

Figure 12–1 A very simple, short-term focused CDCo presentation-level model.

Occasionally, we have deviated from architecture modeling standards (standard components, standard symbols, etc.) when creating presentation-level models. The most compelling case for this has been when the organization already has some sort of widely publicized graphical model of target or end state vision. In those cases, we have created an additional *transition model*—one that translates the organization model to a standard conceptual model and then presents both models. (In all the following steps (Level 0 on), we use only *standard* models.)

In addition to a presentation-level model, be sure to hand out a one-page list of recommended key projects with estimated time, costs, and benefits. We have found that the presentation-level architecture model and the architecture project summary are the two most important documents you can construct to have a meaningful discussion with the executives. Figure 12–2 is a sample key project summary for CDCo.

You know the detailed work—at many steps—that was required to create this summary, but we imagine that you too have been exposed to the bottom-line nature of the questions posed by key decision makers and purse holders. That is what we are addressing by preparing the summary.

CDCO KEY PROJECTS FOR 2000	COST	BUSINESS DRIVER
1. Link CDCo & Bookseller Customer Information	$2.3 Mil.	Improve CRM & Targeting
2. Consolidate CDCo Website into Bookseller Website	$0.8 Mil.	Leverage e-Business Channel
3. Develop Combo Offers	$0.1 Mil.	Enhance Revenue
TOTAL	**$3.2 Mil.**	

Figure 12–2 A prioritized architecture-project summary.

The following are a few more presentation hints.

- While your architecture may encompass a long-term view, focus the presentation-level model and the discussion on the current or next budget/business plan cycle. Showing your five-year plan may not only be off-putting for the executives, but it may also put you off your job.

- Structure the presentation to invite interaction. Have planned questions to ask the executives (e.g., "Do you know how many new databases (or applications, etc.) were built last year?"). The goal here is to increase consciousness and create buy-in rather than inviting boredom and headaches.

- Always include *next steps* that require a response and action from the executives (e.g., funding to investigate a new technology, formal support to form an architecture council, etc.). This provides them with a concrete way to be involved and demonstrate support.

Gaining Support from IT

I have known some architects who did not believe that it was necessary to *sell* the architecture to IT. Not only does broad ownership breed success, but it only takes one creative developer to undermine any project through which architecture is implemented. Sometimes it is more difficult to persuade IT to accept the target architecture than it is to persuade the executives—even when the architecture is funded! The following points show why.

1. Resistance to change is natural, normal, and neutral.

   Separate resistance to change from resistance to architecture. Do not take it personally when your efforts elicit skepticism or negative comments. In fact, expect them. Once I learned that the average *sale* took approximately seven tries to succeed, I not only expected, but allotted, time for a few rounds of rejection!

2. You set architecture standards for IT.

   The Toolkit framework requires that we set standards for data, applications, platform technology, and people—and standards are not always followed. Most IT professionals understand the benefits of standards, but when caught between standards and delivery timeframes, timeframes often (always?) win out.

3. Now you must implement architecture standards via IT.

   Popularize standards. Developers love to *belong*. Make them part of the *in-crowd* by sharing the architecture with as many groups in IT as you can. If it works in your organization, we strongly recommend that architects and developers join forces to create the transition documents (e.g., conceptual data model, target system/application flows). At the very least, engage the development organizations by doing architecture presentations, making copies available, encouraging questions, listening, and providing architecture giveaways and incentives.

4. Then, just when you thought it was safe, you will have to enforce architecture standards in IT.

   Even if your IT organization is now likely to follow standards, it is critical to promote architecture compliance by commissioning a governance team or council (e.g., a Standards Team or an Architecture Council that reviews development products for architecture compliance).

When you meet with developers to walk through the architecture, here are a number of suggestions to consider.

- Discuss early versions. Set up meetings when you have a first or second draft of the architecture documents. Key players in IT may have valuable input you will want to include in later versions.
- Request additional volunteers—*teams of experts* or key IT stakeholders—to review ongoing versions of the architecture. Have the teams help create missing documentation, discuss priorities, etc.

- Bring the following documentation to meetings:
  - A key or legend for architecture models;
  - A list of proposed projects and links to gaps, opportunities, and target business state documents;
  - An estimated time and cost for each project—or use documentation review meetings as an opportunity to get help with this;
  - Business benefits for each project; and
  - Suggested implementation priorities.
- If the audience is small enough, you may also want to include complete content for Toolkit framework cells.
- Ask for, listen to, and collect feedback.
- Keep IT in the loop—send updated architecture documents to all participants (or make them easily available, for example, on an architecture website).
- Bottom line—practice becoming a salesperson. Believe in the architecture you are developing. If you are not committed to and not a strong champion of the architecture, you may be in the wrong job.
- Preview new or interesting parts of the architecture plan with key opinion leaders and potential business sponsors.
- Schedule interim reviews with the steering committee.
- Charge the architecture team to broadly share the architecture package. Be as open and communicative about the plan you are developing as possible. Share it with anyone who expresses an interest.
- Do not forget to provide rewards to the architecture team. This is often a more thankless and less instantly gratifying IT job than many others. Reward the team so well that the most talented people want to join your team.
- Every time you have an opportunity to discuss the architecture with a group, take advantage of the opportunity. Reward participants.
- An architecture package or presentation can be very dry. Use your creativity to keep the package interesting.
- Set up presentation opportunities to practice for the *big one*—your executive presentation. This will help you to understand and field the common questions that the material raises. Reward attendees.

Suggested Exercise

List some key opinion leaders whose support you need. How will you get it?

The Toolkit Implementation Framework: Compliance and Other Key Processes

We are about to enter the "softest" sphere of architecture concern. We have discussed the politics around resistance to change (sometimes, a pretty "hard" area). Now we want to discuss some other "people" areas—key supporting processes and the staff who use them.

In most organizations the architects do not control the IT budget. Yet their chief contribution to the business is the creation of an architecture plan that should guide the development of the product and service portfolio (and associated dollars) delivered by the IT organization to support the business in the most budget-conscious way. And, of course, even clearly defined projects can be implemented in ways that seriously compromise the architecture (No!) and add zeroes to the budget.

149

Some of the most effective approaches to use for ensuring that architecture positively influences development are:

- Sanctioned, repeatable architecture processes
- Standardized, accessible architecture outputs
- Clear relationships with other IT processes

By "process" we mean the set of repeatable steps, followed by one or more people performing defined tasks toward the accomplishment of a work objective. Processes have inputs upon which process steps are performed to result in process outputs.

In this chapter, we will look at how to develop an effective architecture governance process. We will also look at some other processes that can provide strong support for architecture success. Agreeing on a repeatable architecture development process greatly contributes to the success of the architecture function. In addition, you will enhance your ability to succeed at architecture by putting in place a standard development life-cycle (SDLC) process, with well-defined roles, artifacts, and clearly defined relationships with the architecture development process.

Architecture Governance Process

By an "architecture governance process," we mean a sanctioned, documented process used by a recognized team on a regular basis to assess the extent to which infrastructure development complies with or deviates from architecture.

The Toolkit IT Framework requires that, as architects, we need to set standards for data, applications, technology, and people. Not surprisingly, standards are not always followed. It is not too difficult to identify and correct violations of "physical" standards (i.e. those affecting technology and people). For example, it is relatively easy to identify if someone is using a nonstandard PC. It is more difficult to detect if an application programmer is writing "spaghetti" code or creating his/her own definition of "customer."

And while most IT professionals understand the benefits of having and following standards, they are caught between following standards and meeting delivery timeframes. Not all business sponsors understand the benefits of standards, but they are often willing learners. If the business sponsors "own" the development budget, they can be terrific allies for implementing standards and extending deadlines, when they understand the trade-offs. They may be able to help you "enforce" standards by tying funding approval to the implementation of standards.

Some good "softer" techniques for selling the use standards to the IT organization include the following.

- Getting IT participation in the teams that set the standards.
- Making standards easily available. We have used "architecture fairs" and an architecture website to promulgate standards with some success.

Even if your IT organization is likely to follow standards, it is highly desirable to have a formal architecture Governance Process to assess and promote architecture compliance. We strongly recommend formally commissioning a governance team or council (e.g., a Standards Team or an Architecture Council, which reviews development products for architecture compliance). We have found that governance, like a multivitamin, is good for pretty much everyone. The governance process actually invites interaction with development, and (eventually) can come to be viewed as valuable input for development. A governance process works best when the following occur.

- A formal process is developed and documented.
- The process includes an exception mechanism.
- The team is staffed with highly skilled and respected individuals who can adequately represent key stakeholders.
- The team meets on a well-publicized, regularly scheduled basis.
- Compliance reports listing outcomes are created and distributed regularly.

"Formalizing" the architecture governance process means that, like any process, the governance process needs to include defined inputs (e.g., "What artifacts will the "defendant" provide?"), defined outcomes and outputs (e.g., "What form will the council's decision take?") and repeatable steps (e.g., "How are decisions made?").

These are highlights from the CDCo architecture governance process:

- Inputs
  - Architecture models
  - Technology and system design models (which is another reason to use a standard symbology—it makes comparison to target easier)
  - Data models (including entity names and definitions)
- Outputs
  - Overall design assessment (e.g., "compliant, noncompliant, exception granted, modifications underway")
  - Findings—written comments identifying problems or suggestions for modifying the design
  - Actions required—what follow-up is necessary (e.g., exceptions require plans to migrate to compliant design within one year)
- Process Steps
  - The IT design proposal is presented
  - Clarifying questions are asked
  - Alternatives are discussed
  - A decision on assessment outcome requires full concurrence of the team
- Logistics
  - The architecture review meetings are scheduled twice monthly
  - Participants are notified via email of which projects will be reviewed at each meeting
  - All participants are notified of the outcome via email
  - A date is set for a review of designs requiring modifications

Because very few events in life are perfect, having an exception mechanism is very useful for communicating about noncompliant proposals. For example, in one case we made suggestions as part of our feedback on a noncompliant design. The designer had not thought of the "architecturally correct" solution and was very willing to change the design. Having an exception mechanism also promotes negotiation. In one "business emergency" situation, we agreed to grant an exception, provided the noncompliant solution included a plan for how the design would later be migrated towards target.

When you do a good job of designing the architecture governance process, you can also use it to measure architecture effectiveness. For example, you can use the set of outcomes (e.g., compliant, noncompliant, exception granted, modifications underway) as the basis for measurement (by counting outcomes, by type, etc.) of projects reviewed within a specific time period. When you report these results, you may notice an interesting side effect. While publishing and distributing regular compliance reports (e.g., monthly) may seem like overkill, in at least two instances we saw the number of "violations" (exceptions) drop dramatically after the reports were distributed a couple of times. In the CDCo example, the CIO publishes the quarterly report via email and distributes it to all department heads in IT, and to the CIO's business peers.

And for a compliance process to be most successful, it needs the support of executive business sponsors and key opinion leaders (e.g., the CIO or executive business sponsor announces the formation of the architecture council, its mission, and membership). Here is the CDCo example:

> The CDCo CIO sent out an email to announce the formation of the CDCo Architecture Council. She commissioned the council to review and rule on IT design compliance with target architecture, included the schedule for review sessions, attached the format of the quarterly report of assessment outcomes, and named the newly selected team members as contacts (whew!).

It is critical to staff the governance team with highly respected individuals. It is also important to have a team in place with the right mix of skills to evaluate all aspects of the proposed design against the architecture. In our CDCo example, the CDCo CIO named one data architect, one application architect, and one technology architect from CDCo and Bookseller, and one CDCo human resources manager, as members of the architecture council.

We have found that implementing a governance process is critical to the success of the architecture—performing a role much like that of physical therapy following surgery. If you do not do one (governance "therapy"), then the original (architecture "surgery") may be ineffective.

Architecture Development Process

A "healthy" architecture development process needs to address several questions.

- What work does an architect do? The scope of architecture responsibility needs to be defined. For example: Do architects create an annual plan? Do they create the architecture for every project? Is there a recognized link between the architects and the enterprise/IT financial planning (e.g., a forum, a funding approval process)? Does the enterprise require the architects to sign off on solutions?
- When are architecture products needed? Are there scheduled architecture deliverables?
- Where is architecture stored or accessible? Is there a repository for architecture? Are there logistics for architects to communicate with each other, IT, and the enterprise (e.g., regular walkthroughs, architecture website)?
- How does architecture fit with the Systems Development Life Cycle (SDLC)? Are the architecture inputs and outputs standardized (e.g., created within an architecture framework, created using a standard representation)?

When Should Architecture Be Developed?

When you first undertake an enterprise architecture, the architects need to create all the outputs we described in the IT framework. In most cases, we recommend that the architecture team create a full update of the architecture at least annually. Quarterly updates are ideal, since the business of the business keeps changing. Earlier we discussed the importance of establishing and maintaining a strong linkage with the business. Where possible, we recommended that this link be formalized (e.g., through quarterly meetings). The meetings really serve two purposes—they allow the business to communicate changes to the architects, and they allow the architects to provide updates to the business. We have already addressed the desirability of presenting the architecture to key business leaders for concurrence. If you can meet quarterly to review the highlights of the updated plan, you will help insure the continued success of the architecture—and the business.

While it may not fit with your current organizational structure, if you can formally join IT financial planning with strategic planning (architecture), your efforts will be even more effective. And, if the work of the architects also includes a review of new projects (e.g., through a governance process) then so much the better. In the best of all possible worlds, the release of funds for budgeted projects would be tied to architecture review. So, where possible, an architect's output should include:

- The IT plan, updated at least annually
- An annual financial plan for IT
- A project architecture assessment
- A quarterly update and presentations

Where Is the Architecture?

The tools that automate the development—or more accurately, the documentation—of architecture are becoming more sophisticated, and we look forward to their maturity. But there is nothing wrong with creating home-grown architecture artifacts. What is most important is that the outputs are consistent, maintained, and published (shareable). If you have a working repository, then that would be an excellent place to store, maintain, and share the architecture. And in many cases we have seen that developing an architecture website or taking advantage of in-place collaborative software allows for effective storage, maintenance, and sharing of architecture outputs.

SDLC Process

We described the key outputs an architect needs to create using the three frameworks—business, IT, and implementation. Following the steps outlined for each output results in a repeatable architecture development process. It can be difficult to influence IT to comply with the architecture; it would be impossible to do so if the architects themselves did not follow a standard architecture development process. Where possible, it is extremely beneficial to include the architecture process in the SDLC methodology. This not only promotes a strong relationship with the development process, but allows for clearly specifying the artifacts that will be exchanged between architects and developers at different steps in the process. Some points at which to consider incorporating architecture tasks into the SDLC include the following:

- *Feasibility or Proposal*   Whatever you call the first step in your SDLC process, it generally includes not only the business problem, but a very high-level solution to the problem. In many cases that we are familiar with, it is a business or systems analyst that proposes a solution—and that solution is very often based on current systems and data, or those with which the analyst is most familiar. Our best recommendation would be to give the architects the responsibility for proposing the high-level solution. If this is not workable in your organization, then we would recommend that the architects have review and veto power here. Where the proposed solution is completely counter to the target architecture, we would expect the architects to propose a more compliant solution. If you believe that the only acceptable way to get the architects involved in feasibility is as part of a solutions team, then at the very least, see if you can introduce this approach.

- *End of Analysis*   At the point at which the systems, data, and technology analysts have proposed a more refined solution (e.g., where the work effort can be more proximately estimated), we would recommend formal architecture review. (See "Architecture Governance Process"above.)

- *Completion of Detailed Design*   If it is possible (based on the size and complexity of your organization), it is highly desirable to have a review of the technical solution before coding begins. It is reasonable to expect that by the time the design is complete, some divergence from the original solution has occurred. The purpose of an architecture review at this point is to ensure that the solution is compliant—at least in spirit—with the target architecture and that any necessary deviations will not have a significant adverse impact on other parts of the infrastructure.

Identifying and defining the key artifacts that architects and developers will exchange is also important because the architects need to provide developers with target plans in an expected, understood format (e.g., architecture models with standard components using standard representation). Developers need to provide architects with designs in expected, understood formats.

Three suggestions for establishing the set of artifacts to be exchanged include:

- The architects publish an architecture output format and specify a standard format for developers to use to create project designs
- The development community follows a standard methodology (e.g., CMM, an industry SDLC methodology, a home-grown methodology) and *design documents* are required and already standardized
- Architects and designers collaborate to determine the minimum set of outputs (content and format) to be submitted for architecture communication/review

We prefer the second or third alternatives, as they are more likely to reduce the conflict reaching this kind of agreement may cause.

Case Study 13–1 is an example of how we linked the CDCo architecture governance process with the system development process.

You may also want to define other points in the SDLC where development products will be reviewed by architecture and what constitutes the review. For example, you might establish a review point after detailed design, and modify the list above to check for adherence to standards versus adherence to logical architecture.

Case Study 13-1 CDCo Example

At the step in the SDLC life cycle where we assess the project feasibility (a very early look at the potential impact of a proposed project on systems infrastructure), the project owner needs to provide, for architecture review, a project proposal that includes a description, draft system, data models or diagrams, major inputs, and major outputs. Specifically, the input will include:

- *Major Functions/Applications* Name of business function (from Target Architecture Model)
- *Data Stores* Entity Name of Data Store (from Enterprise/Conceptual Data Model) including proposed files, databases, data warehouses, data marts, identification of appropriate data source
- *Key Interfaces* Name of Interface, including users, customers, systems, external sources
- *Information Flows* Entity Name (from Conceptual Data Model)
- *Network Connectivity* Name of type of connectivity required (e.g. LAN, WAN, IP, etc.)
- *Metrics Requirements* High-level view of planned measurements (e.g. identification of support, error management, trouble reporting, audit/control points)
- *Performance Requirements/Budget (High-Level)* For example: required response time, estimated transaction volume, concurrent users

The architecture review results in refined project proposal (may be more than one alternative).

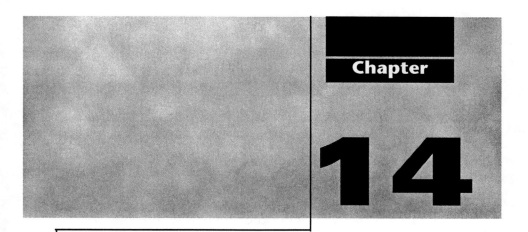

The Toolkit Implementation Framework:
People

Human Resources Issues for Architecture

In our recent planning work with medium- to large-sized organizations, we have found a heightened interest in the softest side of architecture—the people. The increase in "the speed of business" has tended to reduce the attention paid to some of the traditional approaches to people management. We have found (more than once) a lack of formal documentation that describes staffing and compensation criteria, objectives, required outputs, and job/role definitions for architects.

Evaluating HR Practices for the Architecture Team

If you are going to take on the job of architecture, it is important to allow for an assessment of current human resource (HR) policies and to identify the need to add or modify HR policies for the architecture team at the same time. In organizations where the term "architect" is a relatively new position, staffing, compensation, and titles or levels are particularly important. They reflect how you want to position architecture—its value and *clout*. There are several areas worth investigating.

- How are candidates chosen to staff architecture jobs? Are they named or selected by individual managers and assessed or certified against a set of skills and knowledge criteria?
- Are there criteria for architect performance evaluations?
- Are there compensation plans for architects?
- Is there an architecture career path and criteria for career progression for architects?
- Do they attend specific training?

To address any gaps, consider the following.

- *Staffing*   Create job/role descriptions that include specific skills and knowledge the candidate must be able to demonstrate (more to come in "Key Architecture Roles" on page 163)
- *Performance*   Establish formal objectives for architecture outputs against which performance is measured—specific criteria, such as the quality and timeliness of objectives output and feedback from the business partners for architect performance evaluation
- *Compensation/recognition*   Investigate special incentives, such as bonus pay, training/education programs, and *perks* for compensation for the *hazardous duty* conditions of architecture work. Since architecture is about as far as you can get from instant gratification, it is particularly important to have rewards and recognition in place to help the architects persevere.
- *Career Paths*   Consider putting in place at least two levels of architect titles (e.g., *associate* and *senior*) because promising, less-senior IT professionals can be trained and mentored by seasoned architects. Define the level of skill and knowledge that differentiates the titles. Broadening the base of candidates helps

fill succession-planning needs. Stay open and be creative in terms of creating a staffing pool for architecture. When someone in IT disagrees with you repeatedly and often makes a persuasive case, for example, you may want to invite that person to join your team.

- *Training/certification* We have worked with organizations that have investigated or developed formal certification processes for architects. If this seems too complex to undertake (and it can be very complex, with all the attendant *political* issues), consider implementing a training path for architects. This can include specific courses and workshops and attendance at broader-based industry conferences (e.g., the METAGroup/DCI Enterprise Architectures Conference).

Staffing the Architecture Team

Architecture has the potential for tremendous positive impact on the business. The task of determining who should be an architect and what his/her contribution will be is a significant responsibility. Organizations that take architecture seriously have answered many or most of the following questions. The answers to these questions can help to identify who the architects should be and what their role is (or should be) relative to the organization. Who is or should be an architect in your enterprise?

- Do they meet staffing criteria?
- Do they fill a defined role/job description?
- Is their relationship to other roles already defined?
- What outputs are they responsible for creating?

In our experience, selecting the architect is just as frequently a *political-appointee* process as it is a criteria-based selection process. You can probably guess that we recommend the criteria-based approach—it reduces the reliance on people and fosters reliance on process.

General Staffing Criteria

In many cases we have seen extremely knowledgeable senior IT staff filling architecture positions. In some cases they were less effective than they could have been because they had underdeveloped *soft* skills, like written and verbal communication and flexibility. Here are some broad, general guidelines for assessing, staffing, and selecting the architecture team. Look for candidates with strengths in all of the following areas or provide training where there are gaps.

- Skills and Knowledge
  - *Business acumen*   A very good understanding of the business
  - *Technical knowledge*   An appropriate, current technical expertise in data analysis, application development, and technology
  - *Translating skills*   The ability to understand and interpret information between the business and the IT community
  - *Communication skills*   Very good written and oral communications
- Management Competencies
  - *Leadership*   The ability to be a strong, proactive champion of the architecture
  - *Flexibility*   The ability to support other groups with any needed hand-off from architecture that facilitates implementation
  - *Salesperson*   The ability to create motivation, excitement, and buy-in for the architecture
  - *Integrator*   The ability to understand and mediate across diverse groups and ideas
  - *Miscellaneous*   A familiarity with human resources, finance, and other company policies and processes
- Experience
  - Systems analysis, design, and development
  - Computer or business operations
  - Strategy and/or planning

The Bottom Line is that you should choose highly skilled and respected individuals to staff architecture jobs. Reward the team so well that the most talented people want to join your team.

Key Architecture Roles

We believe there are key roles that influence the success of the architecture. We have looked at how some organizational changes can facilitate building and implementing target enterprise architecture while helping to avoid some of the costly mistakes we described at the beginning of this book.

The following are some symptoms that may indicate the need for organizational shifts.

- There are no IT plans or plans are not tightly linked to the business.
- Where plans exist, there are planning *stovepipes*—a lack of common focus and integration across data, technology, and application plans.
- There are no clear deliverables or accountability where the *IT Architect* title exists.
- The architects are viewed as the ivory tower folks—or worse, as irrelevant fluff.

Our prescription is straightforward but requires management and individual commitment to implement. It is based on clear role definitions, defined outputs, and a forum for communicating. Much like the successful house-building team, the architect, the data, and the application and technology planners need to forge strong relationships based on a common plan, frequent communication, and clear responsibilities. Working together with the business client, they can have a profound impact on IT implementations and ultimately on business success (in which they most likely have a stake).

While it may be surprising, we have encountered more than one situation where the architect was not responsible for any output. In our consulting practice we have developed descriptions for architecture roles and expected outputs for our clients. Here are descriptions of some of the roles we have found to be critical to the ultimate success of the IT organization:

- Information Steward
- Chief/Integration Architect
- Data Planner

- Application Planner
- Technology Planner

The number of people needed to perform the roles, when the roles should be split or combined into jobs, and role placement in the organization often depend on other factors not addressed here (politics). Depending on the size and complexity of your organization, one person may perform part of one role or more than one role. You will note, however, that we have suggested linkages between the roles and linkages with some key processes.

Information Steward

The role of the information steward is to provide end-to-end business ownership of key organization information, to set goals and priorities for the critical IT initiatives that enable the business goals, and to facilitate decision making/problem solving with regard to key initiatives. This position provides guidance and direction for the IT governance process and ideally reports to a business unit head. The information steward is responsible for the delivery of key IT initiatives and their associated business benefits.

Chief Integration Architect

The role of the integration architect is to provide the plan for the organization's information and the applications and technology that process the information. The chief architect works with the business (e.g., information steward) to formulate IT policies and plans that support the enterprise, reduce costs, and leverage the use of existing assets. The architect also works across the IT organization to ensure architecture compliance, conflict resolution, and effective implementation. The architect chairs the IT governance forum and ideally reports to the chief information officer. This position is responsible for delivering, publishing, and maintaining the organization's information technology strategy and conceptual architecture models, and for delivering cost savings as specified in annual objectives.

Data Planner

The role of the data planner is to translate conceptual architecture models to logical data models, define key data standards, and recommend standard data practices (e.g., modeling methods, metadata strategy/repository tools). The data planner is a voting member of the IT governance forum and, ideally, reports to the chief architect. This position is responsible for delivering conceptual data models that embody the architecture and for new projects and logical data models that translate the architecture into input for system and database design.

Application Planner

The role of the application planner is to translate conceptual architecture models to decoupled, reusable, functional services (chunks of code) and to recommend standard application development practices. The application planner is a voting member of the IT governance forum and, ideally, reports to the chief architect. This position is responsible for delivering conceptual application models and for new projects and logical application models/flows that translate the architecture into input for system and database design.

Technology Planner

The role of the technology planner is to translate conceptual architecture to common architecture services and technology plans, to define a standard technical environment, and to select standard platform components. The technology planner is a voting member of the IT governance forum and, ideally, reports to the chief architect. This position is responsible for delivering a technology plan, including platform standards that enable architecture implementation.

We have also provided organization models for some organizations, and we will discuss them shortly.

Data Management Roles

Because our philosophy is somewhat data-centric, and because we have sometimes focused on the data architecture specifically, we have also developed descriptions of some of the roles we have found to be critical to the success of data architecture. The architecture-related data roles we include here are:

- Data Architect
- Data Integration Services
- Data Acquisition Management
- Data Modeler

The following is a discussion of their part in the architecture governance process.

Data Architect

The role of the data architect is to provide the plan for the organization's data. The data architect works with the business (e.g., data stewards) to formulate data policies and plans that support the organization's information, reduce costs, and leverage the use of existing assets. This position works across the IT organization to ensure effective data implementation, data architecture compliance, and conflict resolution. The data architect is a voting member of the architecture governance forum and, ideally, reports to the chief architect. All organization data (databases, data warehouses, reference data, files, externally acquired data, etc.) with emphasis on mission-critical common data are in scope. The data architect is responsible for delivering, publishing, and maintaining the information strategy (policy/principles), the information architecture, and the conceptual data model, as well as delivering costs savings as specified in annual objectives.

Data Modeler

The role of the data modeler is to create logical models, define key data standards, recommend metadata strategy/repository tools, and identify central reference data. Ideally, this position reports to the data architect. The scope of this position includes core organization data as directed/prioritized by the data architect. The data modeler is responsible for delivering logical data models and standards, logical reference-table design, and common repository tools.

Data Integration/Common Data Services

The role of data integration is to identify, describe, and specify the key, common services that need to be built and used across organization applications. This position is a key participant in the construction of the organization's target architecture. The incumbent works across organizations to provide consultation and assure that the services are implemented according to the target architecture. The scope of this position includes all common data services that are identified in the target architecture. This position is responsible for delivering the integration strategy (e.g., Enterprise Application Integration (EAI) strategy) and designing specifications for common services to be implemented. This position is responsible for delivering the cost savings associated with the implementation of common services as specified in annual objectives.

Data Acquisition Manager

The role of the data acquisition manager is to manage the quality and use of data external to, and required by, the organization to ensure support for the organization's enterprise goals, reduce vendor costs, and leverage the use of external data. This position is the organization's advocate for external data and works across the IT organization to ensure effective, compliant interfaces with external data. This position may report to the chief architect. The scope of this position includes all of the organization's external data (e.g., credit bureau data). This position is responsible for delivering, maintaining, and distributing the plans for managing external data. The incumbent is responsible for delivering cost savings resulting from the consolidation of sources and/or improved data quality and vendor agreements as specified in annual objectives.

Complete job descriptions can be found in Appendix G.

Organization Structure

In many cases organizational structure can indicate the degree of support (or lack thereof) for architecture and what value the organization places on it. We have seen organizational structures that disperse responsibility for architecture so pervasively that the likelihood for success is tremendously weakened. In other cases we have seen structures that focus more on technology than on the business and, thereby, undermine the potential value that a more broad-based approach can provide. We have worked with organizations that have been so deeply committed to architecture that they were willing and able to make structural changes. Here are a few questions you can use to evaluate how effectively architects are placed in the structure of your organization:

- Are they members of just one work group, or do they exist in each organization or department?
- Do they take direction from one or more leaders?
- Are they placed high enough in the organizational hierarchy to have any impact?

Where possible, we recommend that all the enterprise architects be placed in a single organization. The communication this fosters can really promote integration. In organizations that are very large, it may make sense to have a single enterprise architecture group, plus local architects in each IT organization who have a matrix (or dotted-line relationship) with the enterprise architecture group.

It is also important to consider to whom the architects report and from whom they take direction. As a general rule, we like to see the enterprise architecture group reporting to and receiving direction from the chief information officer (CIO).

While organizational structure alone will not determine the success or failure of architecture, some organizational realignment can be helpful in getting the architecture well-positioned and underway. In general, a good organizational design is much like a good application design, with high cohesion and loose coupling. What this means for architecture is that, wherever possible, it is a good idea to have complete, single-purpose functions (rather than mix-and-match) with a clear focus, high cohesion, and clean, single-point lines of decision-making authority (low coupling.)

The following are a few other factors we look at to determine if and how the organizational structure might benefit from modification:

- The degree to which change and disruption are tolerated and desirable
- The climate for centralization or decentralization
- The extent to which the organization is hierarchically focused

In Figure 14–1 we have modeled an organizational structure that might be typical when functions are very decentralized and disruptions are not very well tolerated or desirable.

If your organization looks a lot like the one detailed in Figure 14–1, you may want to get help from a higher power before you start creating architecture outputs—at least help with putting a governance process in place.

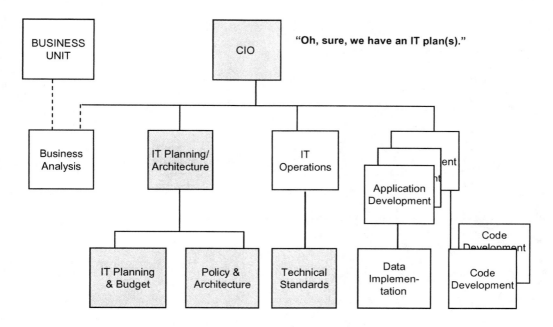

Figure 14–1   Organizational structure #1.

In Figure 14–2, we have modeled an organizational structure where change and centralization are more easily tolerated and where architecture is considered to be a moderately valuable function.

In the type of structure shown in Figure 14–3, you can expect to achieve at least modest success.

In Figure 14–4, we have modeled an organizational structure that might be most suitable for a highly centralized organization with a strong focus on hierarchy, and where architecture is believed to be an extremely valuable function.

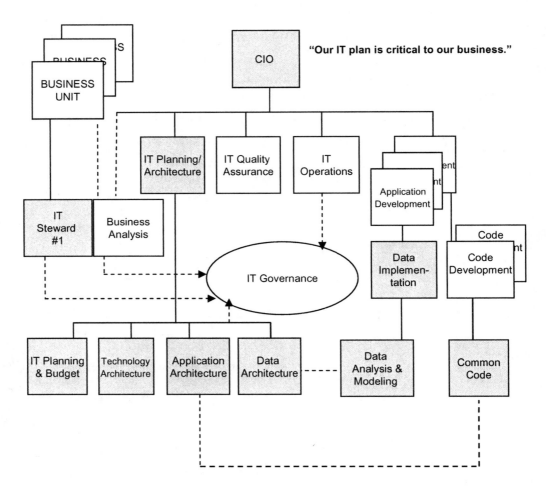

Figure 14–2 Organizational structure #2.

In practice, any of these structures can work if there are other demonstration of strong commitment to architecture. In general, however, we have found that the more centralized architecture functions and well-placed reporting relationships tend to predict greater success, primarily because they demonstrate to the organization that the architecture function is valued.

Of course, neither good organizational design nor great IT human resources policies are silver bullets. We have seen, however, that IT

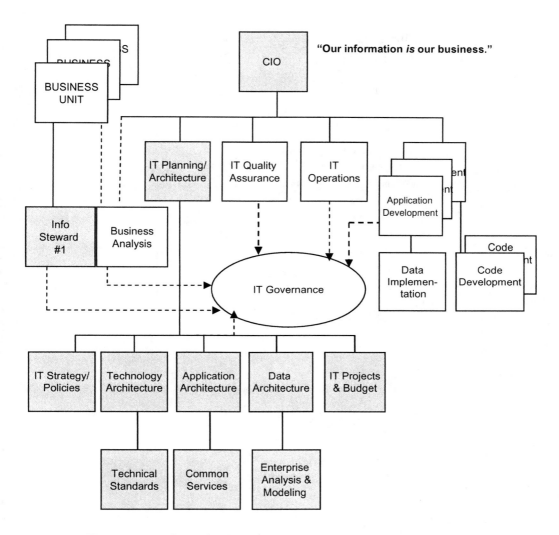

Figure 14–3 Organizational structure #3.

implementations stand a much better chance for success when they include the following traits.

- The business has a clear role in IT planning and business plans are clearly communicated to IT up front.
- The architect is clearly responsible for translating the business plans into cost-effective IT plans.

- The IT plans bring the people-planning function together with the data, applications, and technology plans.

- There is a formal communication channel (i.e., governance process) for cooperatively surfacing and resolving conflicts among all the stakeholders, for evaluating changes, and for providing consistent guidance.

We will address the people issues last—not because they are less important (they are critical), but because we think they can be placed in the best perspective after we have examined all the other key pieces in the framework for implementation (see Figure 14–4).

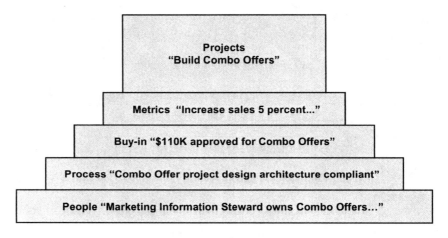

Figure 14-4 Putting it together—framework for implementation.

Putting It Together

Now that we have journeyed all the way from where the business wants to be to how we can staff and organize architecture jobs to support the accomplishment of those goals, let us take one more look at the role of the three frameworks (see Figure 14–5). We used the business framework to collect and organize business needs and goals. We translated these to architecture principles and models and created supporting inventory and standards using the architecture framework. We then greatly enhanced our probability of success by following the framework for implementation—we translated the architecture to realistic projects,

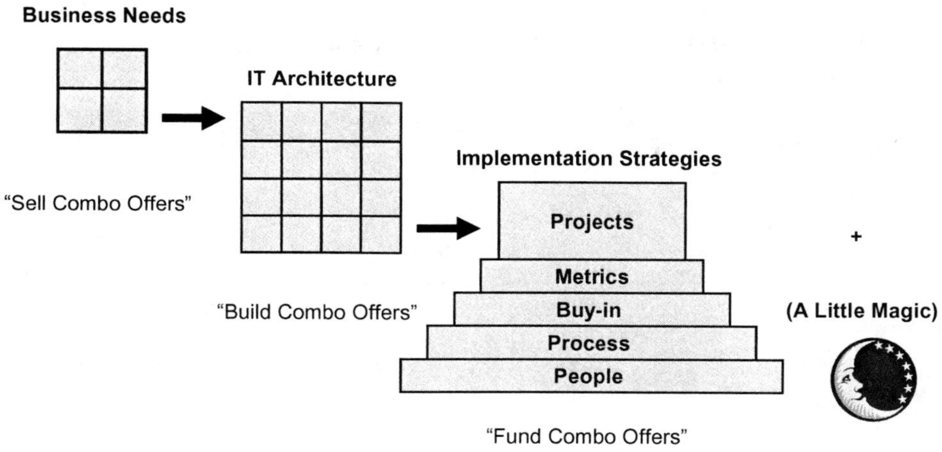

Figure 14-5   Putting it together—infomajic Toolkit.

developed business-focused metrics, sought leadership buy-in and funding, improved our processes, and put the right people in place to run them.

In our workshops students have told us that sometimes the whole process is not entirely clear until we followed it all the way through (see Appendix H for workshop description). For that reason we provide the next and final diagram (Figure 14–6), which illustrates one of the key CDCo business target state needs we uncovered—the capability to sell new or combined offers, the architecture models and standards we developed to create IT plans that include that capability, and the practical implementation steps we followed that enable that capability to be delivered.

A Final Word

So now you know the truth—there is little magic and a lot of hard work required to create and implement target architecture for your enterprise. While the work we have described is challenging, we know from experience that it can be done, and in a relatively short time, by a dedicated, knowledgeable team.

In our workshops we often wish we could tell our students that there are easier ways to undertake the magnitude of change we have been

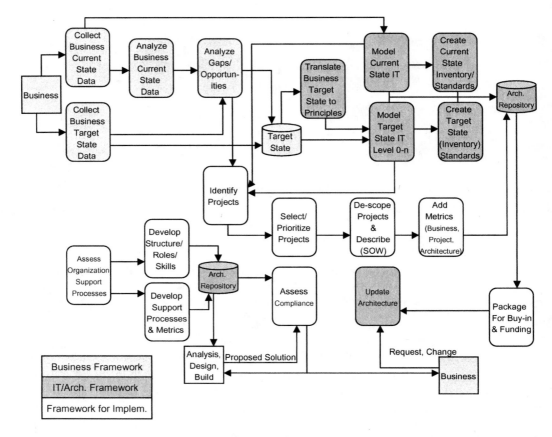

Figure 14-6   The Toolkit process flow.

discussing. What we can tell them is that, while the effort is sometimes extremely challenging (we believe perseverance to be the number one required trait of successful architects), creating and implementing architecture can be tremendously rewarding. We hope you have found the ideas presented here to be useful. On your journey to the target, you can have a profound impact on the achievement of enterprise goals. So, we wish you success, support, and bon voyage in this exciting, demanding, and ultimately rewarding world of enterprise architecture!

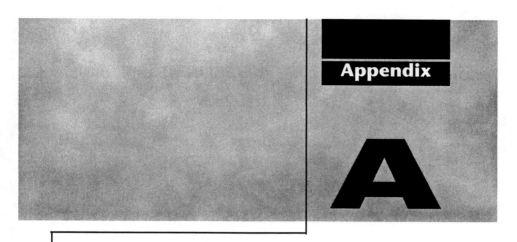

Business Framework Interview Outlines

KEY   Group 1 = Officers/Key Business Experts, CIO
Group 2 = Key Opinion Leaders (Business, IT)
Group 3 = Key IT Leaders

Group 1 Questions

As an Officer of (organization):

1. What is (organization) vision/mission?

2. What is CIO vision/mission?

3. What are (organization)/CIO goals/objectives?

4. What are this year's key business initiatives/major programs?

5. Identify longer-term stress points or risks in the IT organization (major concerns).

6. Identify the strengths and weaknesses of the (organization) business (e.g., skill deficit, low

turnover). These are characteristics for which the organization is known.

7. List the major current (short-term) challenges the organization faces.

8. List the major environmental changes (organization) IT faces, (e.g., new technology).

9. What are potential growth/expense reduction opportunities to which (organization) IT could contribute?

10. Describe significant "history" or changes in business direction (e.g., e-business, mergers and acquisitions, consolidations, deregulation, new ventures, new technology).

11. Describe the (organization) "culture" and identify the major themes or motivational forces that impact the behavior of the organization.

12. Identify key constraints (e.g., regulatory, legislative, shareholder considerations).

How would the business behave if:

- Stress points were relaxed/risks mitigated?
- Weaknesses were addressed and strengths fortified?
- Challenges were resolved?
- Environmental changes were accounted for?
- Growth/expense reduction opportunities were leveraged?
- The "world was perfect?"

Group 2 Questions

As a Key Opinion Leader:

1. Identify longer-term stress points or risks in the IT organization (major concerns).

2. Identify the strengths and weaknesses of the (organization) IT business (e.g., skill deficit, low turnover). These are characteristics for which the organization is known.

3. List the major current (short-term) challenges (organization) IT faces. You can often tell a challenge by the fact that several different groups are working to address it.

4. List the major environmental changes (organization) IT faces (e.g., new technology).

5. What are potential growth/expense reduction opportunities to which (organization) IT could contribute? You can sometimes recognize a potential growth opportunity by the fact that a new idea or "buzzword" has cropped up and everyone wants to be associated with it.

6. Identify organization size in annual expenses and number of employees by organization (e.g., Marketing, IT).

7. List number and types of customers.

8. List users/customers of IT.

9. List locations served and serving.

10. List key products and services.

11. List high-level organization structure and process flow.

12. Show organization structure for IT.

13. Show processes/flow used for CIO.

14. List sales channels (website, call centers, etc.).

15. List key partners/suppliers/vendors.

16. List key reports or indices.

How would the organization/IT behave if:

- Stress points were relaxed/risks mitigated?
- Weaknesses were addressed and strengths fortified?
- Challenges were resolved?
- Environmental changes were accounted for?
- Growth/expense reduction opportunities were leveraged?
- The "world was perfect?"

In the "ideal" future:

1. How will customers and suppliers interact with us (e.g., "Suppliers will accept our orders electronically.")?

2. What will the future high-level business function flow look like?

3. What key business information will flow through the process?

4. What critical people plans and skills will be in place (e.g., "There is a single, cross-trained IT organization.")? What critical support processes and structures will be in place (e.g., "The new skills assessment process is used by all managers.")?

5. What key enabling capabilities will enable the desired state (e.g., "We have the capability for a customer with a service problem to reach a live agent from the web site.")?

Group 3 Questions

As an IT leader/manager, please describe:

1. Number and types of customers

2. Users/customers of IT services

3. Locations served and serving

4. Data center/storage/distribution locations

5. Network and user locations

6. High-level organization structure and process flow

7. Organization structure for IT

8. Processes/flow used for IT

9. Key suppliers/vendors

10. Key reports or indices

11. Indices/measures for IT

12. Current technology:
    - Network, servers, and operating systems
    - Communications services—pair-wise interfaces, APIs, messaging, etc.
    - Development/analysis tools
    - External interfaces (e.g., external systems & databases)
    - Data management software—extraction/cleansing/mapping, DW/DBMS, repository, modeling, etc.

13. Major applications (CRUD) and databases

Key Data Collection Documents

Business Framework Data Collection Documents

- Mission/goals statements
- Strategic and operational business plans
- Key business initiatives/major programs
- Business unit/IT organization charts
- Research, trade publications
- Major program objectives
- Target business process flows
- Current organization assessments
- Annual IT plan/key initiatives
- IT process flows
- Measurement result reports
- Supplier agreements
- Target function flows
- Target information flows
- Target process requirements
- Formal process descriptions

Architecture Data Collection Documents

1. Current architecture
   - Execution environment
   - Operations environment
   - Tools/development environment
2. Repository documents
   - Architecture, models, design documents, application system/data flows
3. Data structures, volume, locations

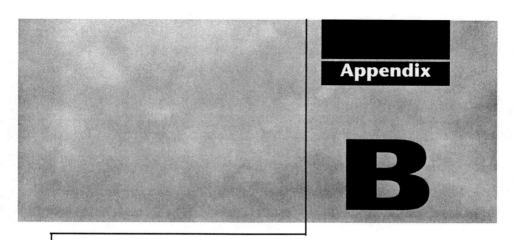

Sample Architecture Principles

Enterprise IT Principles

- The *Business* drives architecture.
- *Information* will be managed according to our Information Policy, as a corporate resource.
- *Functions* will be reusable and reused.
- A single system development life cycle (SDLC) methodology will be employed for all systems' development efforts.
- Application development *Tools* will be consolidated and versions standardized to reduce rework.
- A bias to *Buy* application functions and tools will exist where competitive differentiation is not a primary driver.
- Purchasing decisions will be aligned with the architecture for network, hardware, training, and software.

- *Communications Services* between architecture components will be message-based.
- All Customer and User Support applications will have a common graphical user interface (GUI).
- All *Workstation* purchases will support the "universal workstation" concept (i.e., the workstation can be used by all employees for all work).
- Where feasible, business execution *Platforms* will be consolidated to reduce costs and improve service.
- Operational tools will be consolidated and measurements will be standardized.
- Up-to-date training and education will be continually provided for our IT staff.
- Quality improvement practices and measures will be employed across IT.

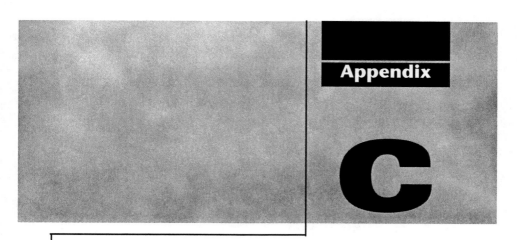

Example Architecture Strategies

Application Development Strategies

- *Analysis and Design*   The outputs of analysis will be directly traceable to the target architecture. Object-oriented or highly structured methodologies will be employed to develop and document the outputs of systems analysis and design for "industrial strength" and mission-critical applications. Analysis and design must include human-factors engineering, which will be responsible to ensuring a common "look and feel" of applications. Where they enhance the methodology, Joint Application Development (JAD) and Rapid Application Development (RAD) techniques may be used. The outputs of analysis and design will be reviewed by architecture for compliance with the target.

- *Prototyping*   Prototyping will be used to support analysis and design in the development of all but very small applications. Where possible, prototyping should employ the graphical tools that will be used to create the production application.

- *Coding*   Application developers will first seek to reuse existing code. Where new functions must be built, they will create small, structured modules or objects that support reuse and inheritance to maximize resource utilization.

- *Estimating*   Function Point Analysis should be utilized for time and cost estimating.

- *Testing*   Structured testing methodologies (e.g., Glenford Myers *flowgraphing*) should be used to assure module/object code accuracy and quality. Integration testing and systems testing should precede end user testing and should also employ structured testing methodologies.

- *Certification*:
  - Design reviews and application walkthroughs should be performed at specific intervals per the SDLC to include development, support, and operation groups within ITS.
  - Production support must sign off on all application changes.

- *Project Management*   All development efforts will be managed and tracked using a formal project management methodology.

Data Management Strategies

- Where possible, single sources of data will be identified and used.
- Data standards will be deployed in any new data stores, messages, and transactions. Legacy data will be evaluated for compliance/conversion to standards.
- No new files, interfaces, databases, warehouses, or tables will be built without explicit architectural approval. Any new data that needs to be created will comply with the target architecture and be incorporated in the Conceptual Data Model.

- Conceptual Data Model updates will be driven by target architecture updates.
- Transactional data will be available for query, analysis, and reporting only through data extraction to an information warehouse. Warehouses will not be used for operational processing.
- Sets of fairly static common table data will be maintained and updated centrally, and periodically distributed to all sites.
- Where technology (DBMS, etc.) provides effective support, data may be replicated. Data replication should be reviewed by the corporate data administrator.
- Data location
  - Cost permitting, when data is accessed and updated primarily at one site, it should be located at that site. When the same transaction data is accessed and updated by users in multiple sites, it should be located in a Data Center site and distributed dynamically. High-usage distributed data should be cached at the client.
- Applications which access client-owned data located at a client site should be available to business function servers through a host-access interface via the corporate network.
- A host data server will normally be co-located with the client's data, unless the data volume, number of users, and required bandwidth make co-location unnecessary.
- Where feasible, the number of database management systems and the number of data warehouse/datamart systems will be reduced to improve cost structure and promote data consistency.
- Messages will be standardized and cataloged. Data administration will "own" messages—determining appropriate industry standards and format.

Technology Strategies

- Communications across architecture components will be message-based (as opposed to direct-connect or Remote Procedure Call). EAI will be implemented via messaging.

- Small- and mid-range *Servers* will generally be used to support office automation, infrastructure systems, and service applications. While mainframe MIP reduction is desirable, larger servers and mainframes will continue to be needed to support high-volume, large-database, customer-centric applications. To the extent possible, the number of different types of servers will be reduced.

- Solutions that are purchased need to comply and/or be compatible with our standard *Platforms*.

- *Network* communications will support a single, open protocol for both peer-to-peer client/server communications as well as LAN work group communications.

- Industry standards will be the basis for Network Computing infrastructure, including standards for naming, IP addressing, and routing protocols, remote network access, and network security.

- *Network Design* will allow for maximum throughput, approaching 100-percent availability, fault tolerance, and room for expansion to accommodate future growth.

- Current LAN switching technology will be incorporated in order to provide high service levels and assist with migrating to ATM and optical standards.

- Secure remote LAN access into our network will be provided and standardized on a single Wide Area Network (WAN) service for communications between all our facilities.

- Industry standards for Network Management will be incorporated by utilizing a standards-based management platform. Network management platforms will integrate voice, data video, and imaging into a common set of management tools.

- All *Technology* standards and updates will be reviewed with the business continuity group for incorporation into and updates to the disaster recovery plan.

Example Target Application Architecture Patterns

This section is an extension of IT strategies.

For new *Applications Design*, architecture consisting of three or more logical application tiers is preferable to two-tier designs. That is, data and data access will be separated from business-function logic, which will be separated from user-interface logic.

- Three-or-more-tier physical architecture should be implemented to support three-tier logical architecture where practical, especially where the system has a large number of users, a large number of transactions, and a life expectancy of greater than three years.

- There are cases where a two-tier architecture makes sense. A two-tier architecture may be used:

  (a) to separate the user interface only (e.g., in the case of legacy migration); or

  (b) to separate the data only (e.g., in the case of a new, very small application).

In the case of (a), a standard GUI tool should be used. In the case of (b), the data should be implemented using a standard DBMS and a standard two-tier 4GL. A small application is defined as one which has less than 100 users, limited complexity (e.g., no Customer Telephony Interface), less than 25 windows, low data transaction volume.

- Systems that support core services should use a standard agent interface (common "look and feel") and incorporate standard services (e.g., error messaging).

In most cases our application design should conform to one of the following models:

- "Industrial Strength"

  - *Assumptions*   Most large, complex mission-critical applications (i.e., supports a customer product or service) will use a three-or-more-tier model (separation of presentation, business function, and data access). The expectation for these large applications is that data will be housed on an "industrial-strength" server.

- Client/Server "Lite"

  - *Assumptions*   Some applications that have a small-to-moderate number of customers and users, and process small to moderate number of transactions, may use a two-tier model (separation of presentation and business function from data access).

- Legacy Surround

  - *Assumptions*   Some existing mainframe mission-critical and business-support applications will be modified to use a two-tier model (separation of presentation from business function and data access). If cycle time can be reduced, applications can be pushed closer to the users. For *Migration* of legacy systems to client-server architecture, when a two-tier logical architecture is used, a "thin" client is preferable to a "fat" client; that is, user interface should be separated from business logic and data. Legacy surround may be used when they provide the most cost-effective solution.

- Buy

  Assumptions New, non-core applications or services will be purchased when there is a function/platform fit available.

- Other(legacy)

  Assumptions The remaining applications, because they are scheduled to be retired or the cost of conversion exceeds the benefit, and little to no support resources are required, may be left to be maximized or "phased out."

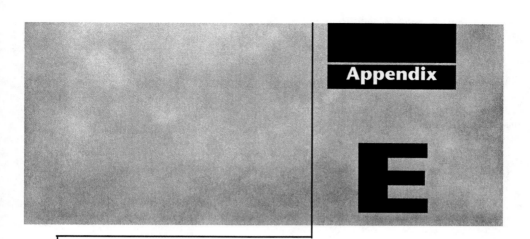

Estimating IT Work Effort for Projects

Sample Scale for Estimating IT Effort

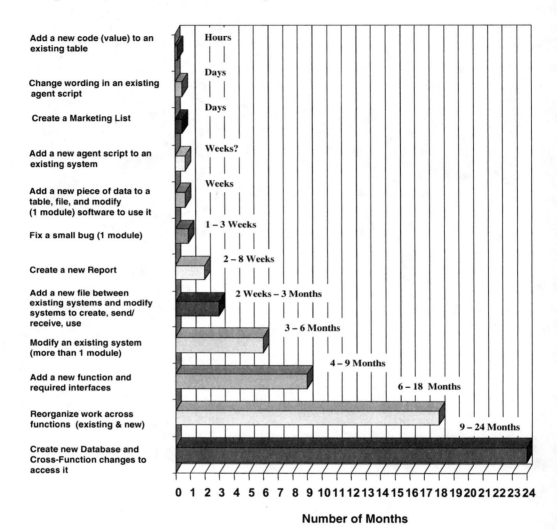

Figure E–1   A sample scale for estimating IT work effort.

Add New Code

Example Add new code to CDCo Product Table

Time Required 5–6 hours

- No coding changes required
- No data structure changes required
- Automated table update process exists

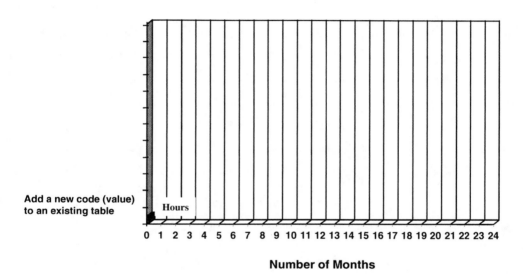

Add a new code (value) to an existing table

Hours

0 1 2 3 4 5 6 7 8 9 10 11 12 13 14 15 16 17 18 19 20 21 22 23 24

Number of Months

Figure E–2 Effort needed to add new code to the CDCo product table.

Change Script—Wording-Only

Example   Wording-only change in CDCo Call Center Sales Script

Time Required   2 days

- No coding changes required

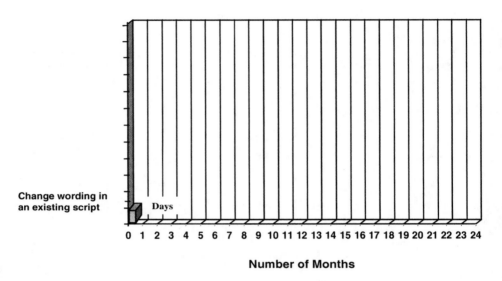

Figure E–3   Effort needed to create a wording-only change in the CDCo call center script.

Create New List

Example   Create a new Marketing List

Time Required   4 days

- Existing process
- Requires data extraction
- No coding changed required

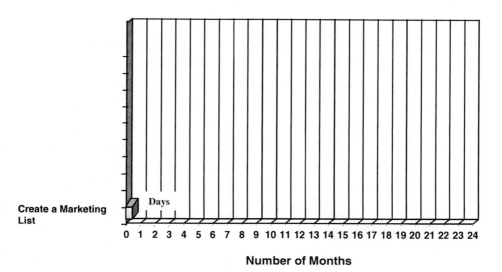

Figure E–4   Effort needed to create a new marketing list.

Modify Existing Script

Example Modify existing call flow script

Time Required 2–4 weeks

- Requires some Human Factors design
- Requires updates to feeds
- May require new edits
- May require additional coding changes

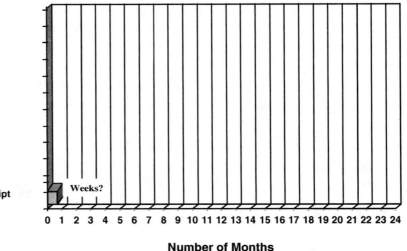

Figure E–5 Effort needed to modify an existing script.

Add New Code—Code Contains Intelligence Used by Applications

Example   Add new code to the current CDCo product code

Time Required   3–5 weeks

- Requires coding changes to multiple systems, feeds, and scripts

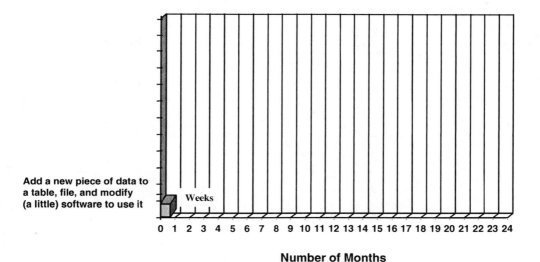

Number of Months

Figure E–6   Effort needed to add new code which contains intelligence used by applications.

Fix Small Bug

Example   CDCo billing S&H calculation error

Time Estimate   3 weeks

- Limited coding changes required
- Limited testing required

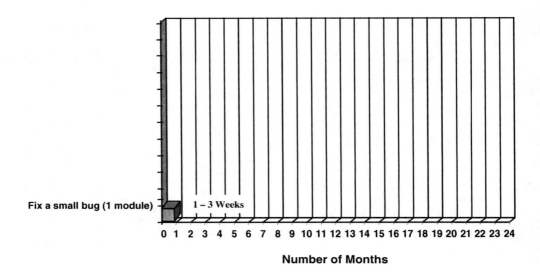

Fix a small bug (1 module)   1 – 3 Weeks

0 1 2 3 4 5 6 7 8 9 10 11 12 13 14 15 16 17 18 19 20 21 22 23 24

Number of Months

Figure E–7   Effort needed to fix a small bug.

Create New Report

Example   Create a new CDCo consolidated financial report
Time Required   6–8 weeks

- Requires design
- Requires testing with partner (Bookseller)
- May require new data
- Uses existing source tables and reporting package

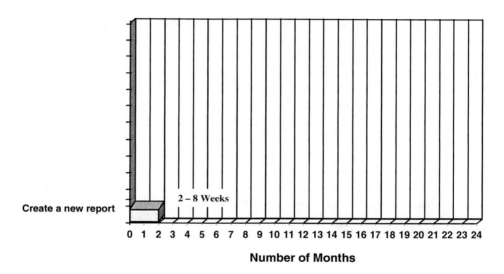

Figure E-8   Effort needed to create a new CDCo consolidated financial report.

Create Customer List

Example   Create a CDCo/Bookseller customer list

Time Required   2.5–3 months

- Requires data definition/translation and analysis, physical design
- Requires coding changes
- Requires cross-partner testing

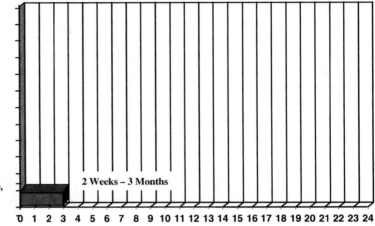

Add a new file between existing systems and modify systems to create, send/receive, use

2 Weeks – 3 Months

0 1 2 3 4 5 6 7 8 9 10 11 12 13 14 15 16 17 18 19 20 21 22 23 24

Number of Months

Figure E–9   Effort needed to create a CDCo/Bookseller customer list.

Modify Existing Applications—More Than One Module

Example Create new combined offers on Web channel

Time Required 3–4 months

- Requires cross-system analysis and design
- Requries coding changes to marketing, sales, fulfillment, and financial systems
- Requires extensive cross-system testing
- Requires new feeds/interfaces

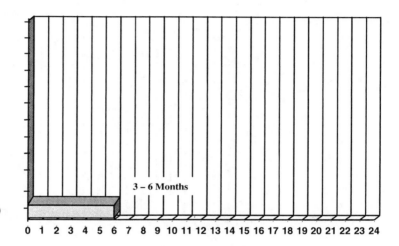

Modify an existing application (more than 1 module)

3 – 6 Months

0 1 2 3 4 5 6 7 8 9 10 11 12 13 14 15 16 17 18 19 20 21 22 23 24

Number of Months

Figure E–10   Effort needed to create a new combined offer on the Web channel.

Add New Function and Interfaces

Example Replace CDCo/Bookseller financial systems and spread-sheets with new consolidated financial reporting system

Time Required 7–8 months

- Requires extensive analysis, design, and testing
- Requires data changes, new interfaces
- Requires extensive coding
- Requires coordination with systems being replaced and/or retired

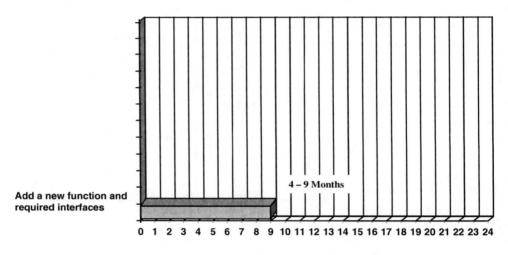

4 – 9 Months

Add a new function and required interfaces

0 1 2 3 4 5 6 7 8 9 10 11 12 13 14 15 16 17 18 19 20 21 22 23 24

Number of Months

Figure E–11 Effort needed to replace the CDCo/Bookseller financial systems and spreadsheets with a new consoditated financial reporting system.

Reorganize Work across Functions—
Existing and New

Example   Redesign cross-partner marketing process (data collection from external catalog and warehouses, new data analysis algorithms, new segmentation scheme and list generation)

Time Required   1+ years

- Requires extensive analysis, design, and testing within CDCo and with external interfaces
- Requries extensive coding, data changes, and interface changes
- Requires coordination across systems and partners/suppliers

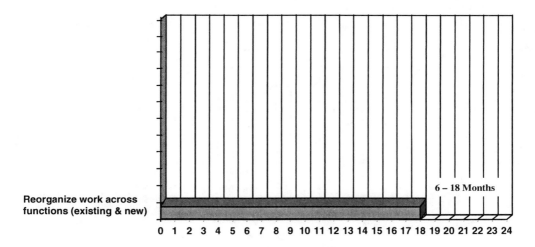

Figure E–12   Effort needed to redesign a cross-partner marketing process.

New Process, Applications, Data Store, and Cross-Function Data Movement

Example   Re-engineer process across marketing, sales, fulfillment, billing, and finance to develop consolidated customer data warehouse with ETL, reporting, analytics, and mining

Time Required   2+ years

- Requires extensive cross-function/partner analysis and design
- Requires new data structures and sources
- Requires massing coding changes within CDCo/Bookseller
- Requires complex testing and migration plans and implementation
- Requires coordination across partners and multiple releases

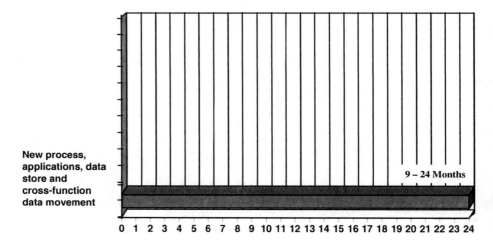

Figure E–13   Effort needed to re-engineer processes across marketing, sales, fulfillment, billing, and finance.

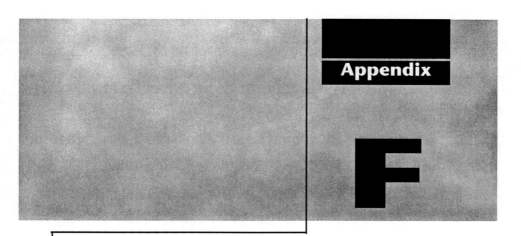

Sample Current Architecture Cost Data Collection

Current Cost of Projects Survey

Thank you for taking the time to reply to the survey. Your input will be extremely useful in quantifying the benefits of architecture/data management at (organization). Please email your responses to _____ by end-of-day _____.

1. **Name of project and brief description** (e.g., Privacy: The purpose of this project is to ensure that all (organization) customer accounts (i.e., mortgage, credit card, other loans) contain the same indication of a customer's desire to share/not share contact information (i.e., address, phone number, email ID) with other list vendors. This project requires that all (organization) customer account files be updated.)

    _____

    _____

_____

_____

_____

2. **Proposed business benefits of project** (e.g., This project is intended to reduce customer complaints by 20 percent, saving the corporation $n in customer representative expenses)

_____

_____

_____

_____

3. **Estimated/Actual project costs**

    a.   Total cost $_____

    b.   Development

           Headcount $_____#_____Person Days_____

    c.   Operational

           Maintenance HC$_____#_____Person Days_____

           DASD/storage $_____

           Transport $_____

           Data acquisition (data purchase)$_____

           Software/licenses $_____

           Tools $_____

           Other $_____

4. **Project architecture**

	Component	New/Existing
Development Language	_____	_____
DBMS (e.g., UBD)	_____	Exist.____
Platform		
OS	_____	_____
Hardware	_____	_____
(Network)	_____	_____
Other	_____	_____

5. **List data flows, outputs, and stores accessed and created**

Name	Created/Accessed	New/Existing	Internal/External	Cost

a. Data Stores/Outputs

(E.g., xyz   Acc.   Exist.   Int. $10K)

_____

_____

_____

_____

b. Data Flows/Interfaces

(E.g., Daily abc feed   Cre.   New   Ext. $50K)

_____

_____

_____

_____

c. If you are unable to break out costs, please estimate the percent of total dollars (3.a.) spent on data (e.g., research, analysis, negotiation/design, acquisition/development, implementation) _____ percent

6. **Contact information**

Name_____

Role _____

Phone_____

(Organization) Location_____

7. **Additional comments on project use/treatment of data** (e.g., roles, processes)

_____

_____

_____

_____

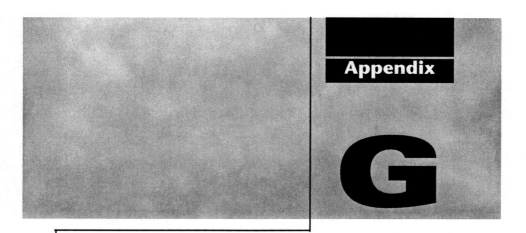

Sample Job Descriptions

Data Steward

Key Functions

The *role* of the data steward is to provide end-to-end business ownership of key enterprise data, to set goals and priorities for the key data, to champion critical data initiatives that enable the business goals, and to facilitate decision-making and problem solving with regard to key data. This position is a key stakeholder in the Architecture Governance Council. It reports to the business unit head.

The *scope* of data stewardship includes oversight of a small set of related data that requires tight management across the enterprise (e.g., Customer Account).

Responsibilities include

Approval of:

- Target architecture
- Core data selection
- Key data standards
- Data sources

Articulation of:

- Business use and cost/benefit/value of data
- Business data quality targets

Expected Outputs

This position is responsible for the delivery of key data initiatives and associated business benefits.

Key Skills/Knowledge

Knowledge

- Deep and broad cross-functional knowledge of the business processes
- General knowledge of information technology capabilities and trends

Skills/Experience

- Senior management experience
- Deep business-process development/management skill
- Extremely strong oral and verbal communication skills
- Extremely strong facilitation/conflict resolution skills
- Advanced degree or equivalent experience

Data Architect

Key Functions

The role of the data architect is to provide the plan for the enterprise data. This position works with the business (e.g., data stewards) to formulate data policies and plans that support the enterprise goals, reduce costs, and leverage the use of existing assets. This position works across the IT organization to ensure effective implementation, architecture compliance and conflict resolution. This position is a member of the Architecture Governance Council. It reports to the IT (chief) architect.

The scope of this position includes all enterprise data (IW, databases, flat files, externally acquired data, etc.) with emphasis on mission-critical common data.

Responsibilities include

Development of:

- An information policy that includes high-level principles around the value and management of the enterprise information asset
- An information strategy that includes, for example, criteria for strategic versus tactical data, a description of the desired use of data for OSS versus MIS functions, an articulation of data integration strategy, and a direction for data consolidation
- A data architecture model and description, including the identification of critical data that is core to the business (e.g., Customer, Account) for stewardship and common management
- A conceptual data model and core entity definitions
- A description of target DBMS characteristics—describing *best fit* data store characteristics
- Determining which data is strategic and should be internally managed, and which data is tactical and can be outsourced

Identification of:

- Duplicate data

Management of:

- Compliance with target data architecture
- Logical data model
- Architecture implementation plans
- Maintenance and publication of policies, architecture, and implementation plans

Expected Outputs

This position is responsible for delivering, publishing, and maintaining the enterprise information policy (Policy/Principles), Information Architecture, and Conceptual Data Model *(and later logical data models/standards/repository)*. This position is responsible for delivering costs savings as specified in annual objectives.

Key Skills/Knowledge

Knowledge

- Deep and broad knowledge of information technology capabilities and trends
- Broad knowledge of enterprise data assets
- General knowledge of cross-functional business processes

Skills/Experience

- Middle management
- Strategy/plan construction experience
- Data architecture/data modeling skills

- Strong oral and verbal communication skills
- Strong facilitation and conflict resolution skills
- Advanced computer science degree or equivalent experience

Data Acquisition

Key Functions

The *role* of this position is to manage the quality and use of data external to, and required by, the business to ensure support for enterprise goals, reduce vendor costs, and leverage the use of external data. This position is the organizational advocate for external data. This position works across the IT organization to ensure effective, compliant interfaces with external data. It may report to the chief architect.

The *scope* of this position includes all external data (e.g., sales lists, credit reports, and compensation studies).

Responsibilities include

- Setting quality standards for external data
- Developing a description of key data sources and acquisition cost/benefits
- Consolidating external data sources where possible
- Interacting with vendors and IT organizations to oversee interfaces with appropriate external data resources

Expected Outputs

This position is responsible for delivering, maintaining, and distributing the plans for managing external data. The incumbent is responsible for delivering cost savings resulting from the consolidation of sources and/or improved data quality and vendor agreements as specified in annual objectives.

Key Skills/Knowledge

Knowledge

- Knowledge of information technology capabilities and trends
- Knowledge of data assets
- Knowledge of business functions
- Knowledge of data management practices

Skills/Experience

- Data analysis experience/knowledge
- Financial/accounting skills
- Vendor relationship management skill
- Technical consulting skills/oral and written communications skills
- Degree in IT/business or related field or equivalent experience

Common Data Services

Key Functions

The *role* of this position is to identify, describe, and specify the key common services that need to be built and used across the organization's applications. This position is a key participant in the construction of the enterprise target architecture. The incumbent works across organizations to provide consultation and assure that the services are implemented according to the target architecture.

The *scope* of this position includes all the common architecture services that are identified in the target architecture.

Responsibilities include

- Identifying common data access/data management services
- Identifying common application functions (e.g., common edits)
- Identifying common communications services (e.g., messaging, transport)
- Identifying common distribution/replication services
- The development of data integration strategy (e.g., logical EAI strategy)

Expected Outputs

This position is responsible for delivering the design specifications for common services to be implemented. This position is responsible for delivering the cost savings associated with the implementation of common services as specified in annual objectives.

Key Skills/Knowledge

Knowledge

- Deep knowledge of information technology capabilities and trends
- Knowledge of data assets
- Knowledge of business functions
- Knowledge of the organization's communications services needs (volume, speed, freshness, etc.)

Skills/Experience

- Data analysis experience/knowledge
- Data communications experience
- Application development experience
- Strategy/planning/architecture experience

- Technical consulting skills/oral and written communications skills
- Advanced degree in IT or related field or equivalent experience

Data Architecture Associate

Key Functions

The *role* of the data architect associate is to assist the data architect, create logical models, define key data standards, recommend repository tools and identify common reference data. It reports to the data architect.

The *scope* of this position includes core enterprise data as directed or prioritized by the data architect.

Responsibilities include

- Data analysis and logical modeling for major new projects
- Developing data standards for core strategic data elements (especially identifiers)
- Developing criteria for repository tool selection
- Assessing and selecting repository tools
- Identifying common reference data

Expected Outputs

This position is responsible for delivering logical data models and standards, a logical reference-table design, and common repository tools.

Key Skills/Knowledge

Knowledge

- Knowledge of information technology capabilities and trends
- Knowledge of data assets
- Knowledge of business functions

Skills

- Extensive data analysis and modeling experience and proven skill
- Proficiency with data analysis tools
- Development experience is highly desirable
- Technical consulting skills/oral and written communications skills
- BA/BS degree in IT or related field or equivalent experience

Enterprise Architecture Toolkit: 3-Day Workshop

Course Description

Course Overview

The objective of this three-day intensive workshop is to equip you and your team to develop Enterprise Architecture. The integrated approach teaches the use of three frameworks designed to help you collect the right information, translate it to infrastructure plans, and implement architecture. The workshop contains architecture development processes and methods that address data, function, technology, and people. It includes specific practical guidelines and the extensive use of examples and exercises. At the completion of the workshop, participants will take away working drafts of architecture outputs.

Target Audience

- IT planners, business planners, architects, and analysts

Course Approach

- Interactive workshop
- Modules include definitions, methods, examples, and exercises
- Focus on output development
- Guidelines—experience-based practical steps to follow in developing the module outputs
- Detailed examples—fictitious company used throughout, so examples build on earlier examples
- Challenging exercise(s)—exercises are based on participant's business or organization
- Brief precourse assignment prepares participant for exercises
- Exercises build on earlier exercises
- Exercises can be done individually or in groups
- Exercise results reviewed and coaching provided
- Integrated approach—audit trail/linkages are identified between/across architecture outputs

Course Outline

0. Introduction:
   - Four architecture scenarios—What worked/what did not
   - Best practices—"What Works"
   - Toolkit overview—Enterprise Architecture "Toolkit" Frameworks

1. The Toolkit Business Framework: Describing the Business Current State

2. The Toolkit Business Framework: Assessing the Business Current State

3. The Toolkit Business Framework: Describing the Business Target State
4. The Toolkit Business Framework: Analyzing the Business Target State—Identifying Gaps and Opportunities
5. The Toolkit Architecture Framework: Principles
6. The Toolkit Architecture Framework: Models
   - General Architecture Modeling Guidelines
   - Detailed Architecture Modeling Guidelines
     - Component-only architecture models
     - Integration architecture models
     - Level 0 architecture models
       - Current state
       - Target state
     - Level 1/n target architecture models
     - Translating architecture models to data models
7. The Toolkit Architecture Framework: Inventory
8. The Toolkit Architecture Framework: Standards
9. Framework for Implementation: Projects
   - Identifying architecture projects
   - Selecting architecture projects
   - Minimizing project scope—six architecture project implementation strategies
10. Framework for Implementation: Establishing Metrics
    - Identifying and defining effectiveness metrics
    - Identifying and defining value metrics
11. Framework for Implementation: Gaining Buy-in
    - Executive buy-in
    - IT buy-in
12. Framework for Implementation: Key Processes
    - Architecture governance and the compliance process
    - Architecture development process
13. Framework for Implementation: Critical People Issues
    - HR policies
    - Key roles
    - Organization structures

Course Logistics

- Delivery of the workshop at your site can be arranged
- For more information, contact:

infomajic llc
14 Sims Avenue
Manasquan, NJ 08736
or
info@infomajic.com

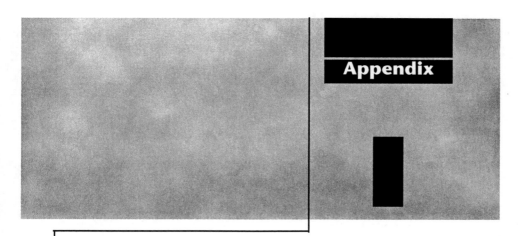

Conducting Enterprise Architecture Assessment: 2-Day Workshop

Course Description

Course Overview

The objective of this two-day seminar is to prepare you with the methods and tools you will need to assess the current state of your enterprise architecture.

The integrated approach teaches the use of three frameworks as tools to help you collect the right information, analyze the information, and translate it into an architecture assessment. The workshop focuses on collecting and creating current state architecture outputs for analysis of the infrastructure—especially data, applications, and technology. It includes specific practical guidelines and the

223

extensive use of examples and exercises. At the completion of the workshop, participants will take away detailed approaches and draft outputs for architecture assessment.

Target Audience

- IT planners
- Business planners
- Architects
- Analysts

Course Approach

- Interactive workshop
- Modules include definitions, methods, examples, and exercises
- Focus on output development
    - Guidelines—experience-based, practical steps to follow in developing the module outputs
    - Detailed examples—fictitious company used throughout, so examples build on earlier examples
    - Challenging exercise(s)—exercises based on participant's business or organization
- Brief, precourse assignment that prepares participant for exercises
- Exercises build on earlier exercises
- Exercises can be done individually or in groups
- Exercise results reviewed and coaching provided
- Integrated Approach: audit trail/linkages identified between/ across architecture outputs

Course Objectives

At the conclusion of this course, you will be able to:

- Understand the value and use-proven strategies for conducting enterprise architecture assessments
- Use the business framework to establish a business baseline by:
    - Defining/collecting key business documents
    - Collecting business interview data
    - Developing process flows
- Use the architecture framework to assess current state architecture by:
    - Defining/collecting key IT documents
    - Collecting IT interview data
    - Refining/constructing current state architecture models
    - Refining/developing current state architecture inventories
    - Assessing current state architecture standards
- Analyze the data:
    - Using SME consensus
    - Using Behaviorally Anchored Rating Scales (BARS)
- Synthesize the data:
    - Considering *soft* issues
    - Summarizing/reporting
    - Making the case for target architecture

Course Outline

1. Introduction
    - Purpose/value of architecture assessment
    - Refresher: the Enterprise Architecture Toolkit
    - The process for enterprise architecture assessment
2. Getting Started: Review of Business Framework
    - Review of "basic" data collection method
    - Detailed guidelines
3. Analyzing the Current State Using the Business Framework

- Review of "basic" analysis method
- Detailed guidelines

4. Collecting Data to Begin Documenting the Current State Architecture
   - Using the Toolkit Architecture Framework for assessment
   - IT interviews
   - Architecture documentation

5. Using Architecture Models to Document the Current State Architecture
   - Review of architecture framework
   - Architecture models
   - Current state architecture models

6. Using Toolkit Architecture Inventory to Document the Current State Architecture
   - Architecture inventory
   - Current state architecture inventory

7. Using Toolkit Architecture Standards to Document the Current State Architecture
   - Architecture standards
   - Current state architecture standards

8. Analyzing the Current State Architecture
   - Problem identification
   - Approaches to analysis
   - Using models and inventory
   - Using BARS with standards
   - SME consensus

9. Summarizing the Current State Architecture in a Meaningful Report
   - Organizational considerations
   - Synthesizing data for summary report
   - Presenting the results

Course Logistics

- Delivery of the workshop at your site can be arranged
- For more information, contact:

infomajic
14 Sims Avenue
Manasquan, NJ 08736
or
info@infomajic.com

Index

229